STARDUST
A QUILT ADVENTURE IN 9 PARTS

EBONY LOVE

Stardust: A Quilt Adventure in 9 Parts

© 2020 Ebony Love. All rights reserved.

AccuQuilt®, AccuQuilt Studio™, AccuQuilt GO!®, Studio™, Two Tone™ and GO!® are trademarks of AccuQuilt. Sizzix®, Sizzix BigShot™, and BigShot Pro™ are trademarks of Ellison. EDeN™ System is a trademark of LoveBug Studios. Use of any trademarks in this book does not imply affiliation or endorsement of the contents by their respective owners.

The book author retains sole copyright to the contributions to this book. No part of this book may be reproduced, stored in a retrieval system, or transmitted in any form, or by any means—electronic, mechanical, photocopying, recording, or otherwise—except for brief quotations for the purpose of review, without prior written permission of the copyright holder.

Every effort has been made to insure the accuracy of information in this publication; should you find any errors, please let us know at the address below and we will post corrections on our website.

Designed by: Ebony Love

Illustrations by: Flaun Cline and Linda Smoker

Edited by: Diane Podgornik

Published by:

LoveBug Studios
1862 E. Belvidere Rd. PMB 388
Grayslake, IL 60030

http://lovebugstudios.com

ISBN 978-1-938889-17-2

Library of Congress Control Number 2019917032

Printed in the United States of America (US Distribution)
1 2 3 4 5 6 7 8 9 10

Contents

Fabric Charts   5

Preparing for Your Adventure   7

Month 1: Starfish & Churn Dash   17

Month 2: Friendship Stars & Churn Dash   23

Month 3: Ohio Star & Flying Geese   27

Month 4: Orange Stars   33

Month 5: Churn Star   41

Month 6: Shooting Stars   51

Month 7: Quilt Assembly 1   55

Month 8: Quilt Assembly 2   59

Month 9: Quilt Finishing   63

Templates   69

Supply List   71

EDeN™ Chart   72

Yardage Chart

Fabric swatch SKUs are from the Primo Collection by Ebony Love and Batik Foundations Neutrals for Island Batik.

Fabric #	Fabric Swatch	Reference Illustration	Yardage
1	311901340	Burgundy	3/8 yard
2	311902025	Lt. Cream	1/2 yard
3	311902360	Pink	5/8 yard
4	311902610	Dark Teal	1/2 yard
5	311902851	Violet	3/8 yard
6	311903060	Gold	1/2 yard
7	311903551	Turquoise	3/4 yard
8	311903849	Mulberry	3/8 yard
9	311903885	Dk. Purple	5/8 yard
10	311904100	Light Aqua	1/4 yard
11	311904502	Med. Aqua	1/4 yard
12	311905065	Orange	3/8 yard
13	311905330	Fuchsia	1/2 yard
14	311905585	Navy	1/2 yard
15	SPRINKLES	Neutral	2-3/4 yards
BINDING	311901585	Midnight	5/8 yard
BACKING	311902725	Med. Grey	4-1/2 yards*

*If you wish to follow the scrappy backing instructions in Month 9 instead, you will need approximately 3¼ yards of backing fabric. You may need more or less depending on the scraps you have remaining.

Please see page 71 for list of recommended supplies.

Fabric Charts

Personal Piece-by-Number Fabric Chart

Fabric SKUs are from the Primo Collection by Ebony Love and Batik Foundations Neutrals for Island Batik.

Fabric #	Fabric Swatch	Reference Illustration	Your Swatch
1	311901340	Burgundy	
2	311902025	Lt. Cream	
3	311902360	Pink	
4	311902610	Dark Teal	
5	311902851	Violet	
6	311903060	Gold	
7	311903551	Turquoise	
8	311903849	Mulberry	
9	311903885	Dk. Purple	

Fabric #	Fabric Swatch	Reference Illustration	Your Swatch
10	311904100	Light Aqua	
11	311904502	Med. Aqua	
12	311905065	Orange	
13	311905330	Fuchsia	
14	311905585	Navy	
15	SPRINKLES	Neutral	
BINDING	311901585	Midnight	
BACKING	311902725	Med. Grey	

You can download a copy of this page from the LoveBug Studios website at:

http://lovebugstudios.com/patternresources/

© 2020 LoveBug Studios. All rights reserved.   http://lovebugstudios.com   cust-service@lovebugstudios.com

Stardust

Preparing for Your Adventure

Before You Begin
It's exciting to start a new project, isn't it? In our excitement however, we are sometimes so eager to get started that we flip past all the introductory information and go straight to cutting.

We'd like to encourage you to take a few minutes and read through this guide so you can familiarize yourself with our writing style, common terms, and get the best advice for success with this pattern.

Skill Level
We don't like to judge anyone or tell you what you can or cannot do. You can be successful making anything if you are willing to learn and are motivated to do so.

That said, knowing how to use basic rotary cutting tools, operate your sewing machine to achieve an accurate ¼" seam allowance (or scant ¼" when called for), and piece efficiently will help you immensely with this pattern. We have some basic instruction within this guide, but if you need more help, consult your local quilt shop, or pop on over to YouTube for a few videos.

Updates and Bonuses
We do our best to make sure the pattern you receive is complete and correct, but sometimes things get past our pattern testers and editors. If this happens, we'll post updates on our website.

We also like to provide additional content for you to access to help you have the best experience possible. Keeping these extras on the website help us to either keep your pattern to a reasonable size, or in the case of books, gives you a way to have copies of charts and templates without destroying the spine of your book.

In all cases, they are on our Pattern Resources page on our website at
http://lovebugstudios.com/patternresources/.

Common Terminology
Quilters have a language all their own and after a while we start peppering our sentences with acronyms and all sorts of weird terms that may be unfamiliar to newer quilters. Here are some common terms and abbreviations you will see throughout this pattern.

> **[ABC-#]** – EDeN Numbers. EDeN stands for Equivalent Die Notation, and it's a way to identify the correct dies for cutting the same sized units. Any abbreviations you see in brackets are instructions for die cutting. If you are rotary cutting, just ignore any instructions in brackets.

HST – Half square triangle. This is a triangle that is made by cutting a square in half across one diagonal. You can recognize HSTs in a pattern because the squares they are cut from will usually end in ⅜" or ⅞".

LOF – Length of fabric. This is the length of fabric along the amount of yardage that you purchased. This isn't a common usage in our patterns, but sometimes it may be specified for sashing or borders.

QST – Quarter square triangle. This triangle is made by cutting a square in half across both diagonals. You can recognize QSTs in a pattern because the squares they are cut from will usually end in ¼" or ¾".

WOF – Width of fabric. This is the width of the fabric from selvage to selvage. It normally measures 42" to 44" for quilting cottons, though it can vary from fabric to fabric due to a number of factors. We assume a WOF of 40" when calculating cuts.

Piece-by-Number

We have numbered each fabric in this quilt from 1 to N, excluding the binding and backing fabrics. Each fabric keeps the same number throughout the entire quilt. In the cutting instructions, you will see a chart that shows the color number and a swatch of the fabric, so that you can follow along with the illustrations.

In the piecing instructions, you will only see the color number referenced. For example, an instruction might say, "Sew (1) Fabric 9 square to (1) Fabric 12 square". That means that this unit uses fabrics 9 and 12 from the chart.

If you are using your own fabric, we suggest creating your own color chart, numbering your fabrics accordingly, and using those fabrics in the same position throughout the quilt. You will find a printable color chart to use on our website.

About the Unit Dimensions

When we give measurements for finished or unfinished units, blocks, and subassemblies, we provide the smallest dimension first, then the largest dimension. That means that a flying geese unit that is 6½" wide × 3½" tall will be denoted in the pattern as a 3½" × 6½" geese unit. When in doubt, refer to the illustrations to show you how units are oriented and which way units should face during quilt assembly.

About the Cutting Instructions

We use bulleted lists to walk you through the cutting of each fabric. Cuts typically start with a major cut—one or more width of fabric (WOF) strips. From these strips, you'll subcut into various types of units. A fabric can have one or more major cuts within the instructions.

If you see indented bullets below a major cut, that means you have more to do with that set of strips. The more indented levels you see, the more you are manipulating that set of cuts, so you should read that instruction fully before cutting.

Here is an example cutting instruction:
- Cut (1) 2⅞" × WOF strip.
  - From strip, cut (12) 2⅞" squares. Cut along one diagonal to make (24) Fabric 7 HSTs. [HST-2]
- Cut (1) 1½" × WOF Fabric 7 strip. [STR-1]
- Cut (1) 2½" × WOF strip.
  - Cut in half widthwise to make (2) 2½" × 20" strips.
    - From one 2½" × 20" strip, cut (6) 2½" Fabric 7 squares. [SQ-2]
    - Set aside remaining 2½" × 20" strip to use in Month 6.

This shows a fabric with three major cuts; you can tell because they are at the first level (not indented) and aligned with the left margin.

The first cut is subcut into HSTs; the second cut doesn't have any additional cuts; and the third has a couple of additional cuts, including what's called a "set aside".

Usually, anything remaining after you cut is assumed to be scrap, but sometimes we can use these leftover fabrics in a later installment. In these cases, we will tell you what to set aside and when you will expect to use it.

Following the above example, when you get to Month 6, you would see this instruction:

- From 2½" × 20" strip set aside in Month 5, cut (5) 2½" Fabric 7 squares. [SQ-2]

We recommend labeling a quart zipper bag for each installment of the quilt; when you are asked to set aside a strip or set of units, use a sticky note to label the fabric, cut size, and installment number and place them in the zipper bag for the designated installment.

About the Pattern Illustrations
The illustrations are visual guides to help you construct the block but should not be viewed as a representation of what your units should look like when you finish sewing them.

In our illustrations, we don't show the outside seam allowances as units are constructed. When you are finished sewing a block, do not trim it to look like the illustration. Your unfinished block has seam allowances that will be taken care of as the quilt is assembled. We give the unfinished measurements of the units and blocks where possible, but if you ever have a question, just contact us and we will help.

Fabric Preparation

No matter what fabric you are using, it's important that you learn a little bit about your fabric and prepare it properly before you start. The following sections cover important tips to help you prepare your fabric in the best possible way to ensure success with your quilt.

To Prewash or Not to Prewash?

Prewashing is a personal choice that is influenced by a number of factors, but whatever you decide, be consistent. If you're thinking about washing the red fabric because you think red tends to bleed more, then you should get ready to wash all of your fabrics.

If you have allergies, respiratory problems, or skin conditions that are aggravated by chemical residue, your health is best served by prewashing.

Cotton fabric tends to shrink in the 3 to 5% range, which amounts to a ½" loss per quarter yard of fabric. What you don't want to do is use fabric that's already shrunk next to a fabric that has more shrinking to do. You may not like the end result.

None of the fabrics for the sample quilt were prewashed, but a color catcher will be added during the quilt's first washing in case any fabric bleeds. If you want to wash your own quilt, please wait until after it is quilted, so you don't have a mess of frayed seams and tangled threads.

NOTE: If you are planning to enter your quilt into a show, it is important that your quilt hang square and straight. In that case, you will want to square your quilt before it is bound in a process called "blocking". This is a more detailed process than we can explain here, but Kimmy Brunner has written an excellent piece on how to block a quilt, and we've linked her tutorial on our Pattern Resources page.

What About Starch and Steam?

If you have prewashed your fabric, your use of starch, water, and steam is up to you. There's little risk of bleeding and shrinking now that you've done that in advance.

If you did not prewash, introducing moisture into your project during construction can lead to undesired results. The best time to use starch and steam is when the fabric is still uncut yardage. Once you start cutting units and piecing blocks, avoid moisture as much as possible so you don't shrink your units and blocks prematurely.

Usable Width of Fabric

The directions assume the usable WOF is 40", even though your fabric may be wider. It is not necessary to cut your fabrics down to 40" wide; in fact, it's a good thing if your fabric has a little wiggle room.

This 40" measurement excludes the selvage. We don't use the selvage for piecing because it is tightly woven, sometimes has large holes, and isn't always printed to the edge. This makes it hard to stitch through and can create inaccuracy when piecing.

For those who wish to save selvages for other projects: you may safely remove them in advance, but leave at least 40" of usable width before you start cutting any strips or units. Keep your fabric folded selvage to selvage as you work so you don't confuse the direction of the fabric grain.

Straightening Yardage

Don't let that crisp bolt-fold fool you! Fabric is rarely folded perfectly on-grain when it is rolled onto the bolt. If you're prewashing, you have to iron the fabric anyway, but if you aren't, you should press out the bolt-fold and straighten your fabric. Here's how.

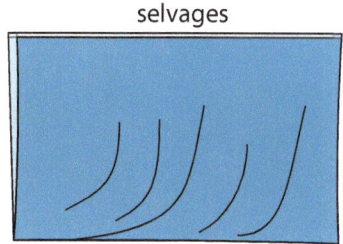

Hold the fabric up by the selvage edges, with your arms away from your body, so you can see the fabric. Don't worry about straightening the entire length of fabric, just the part you can comfortably hold.

When you do this, you may notice the fabric has a slight twist. That's what we need to eliminate.

Keeping the selvage edges aligned as straight as possible, slide or shift one selvage to the left or right until the twist disappears.

 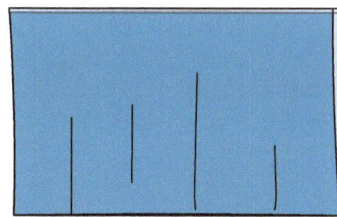

After the twist disappears, carefully lay your fabric onto a cutting surface. Align an inch mark of a long, wide ruler along the bottom fold, and cut off the uneven raw edges. You now have a straight edge for cutting strips.

After making a few cuts, consider straightening your yardage again, especially if you weren't able to straighten the entire length of yardage the first time.

Working with Directional Prints

A directional print is any print that looks different based on the direction it is cut. A row of baby ducks, for example, might be sideways or upside down depending on how you cut and piece them into a block, and this can make a difference in the look of your finished unit.

Preparing for Your Adventure

Because we use solid colors for illustrations, we don't generally give guidance on how best to handle directional prints. With our quilt samples, we just piece what we cut, and units land where they will. Anything more is up to you and your level of obsession with linearity.

If it would bother you to have text reading sideways, or baby ducks upside down, or herringbones facing opposite directions, you may need to take a little more time planning your fabric placement before you begin piecing your blocks. If you are determined to have all your fabric oriented in one direction throughout the quilt, you may need to cut more pieces than we specify in the patterns in order to select the ones that are oriented correctly. This may also require more fabric.

Cutting Tips

Whether you are rotary cutting or die cutting, it's important to remember: safety first!

If You are Rotary Cutting

- **Use a new blade.** When was the last time you changed the blade on your rotary cutter? If you have to press down hard in order to make a cut, it's time. Using dull blades is dangerous, and causes deep grooves in your cutting mats that are less likely to heal.
- **Always cut away from yourself.** This gives you more control over the tool and is safer too.
- **Hold the ruler firmly.** Don't put your hand flat on the ruler; instead, tent your fingers and press down on the ruler as you make the cut. Keep your fingers away from the edge.
- **Don't cross your arms.** You should cut on the same side of your body as you hold the rotary cutter.
- **Close the cutter EVERY TIME you put it down.** It may feel like a waste of time, but it's easy to slice your hand open or lose a toe from a dropped or open cutter.
- **Wear closed-toe shoes.** In the event you forget to close your cutter, or drop the scissors, you can keep all your toes.

If You are Die Cutting

- **Outline your dies.** Do you know where the blades are? They are embedded in the foam in narrow slits that you can barely see. Outlining your shapes shows you where it's safe to put your fingers.
- **Draw registration marks on your dies.** The registration marks will help you align the grain of your fabric with the shapes on your dies. If you don't know how to do this, visit the Pattern Resources page on our website for links.
- **Use both hands.** It's tempting to just pick up a die with one hand, but what if you misjudge the weight, or don't get a firm grip? If you drop a die, let it fall and get out of the way. Resist the urge to grab at a falling die. You might grab it in the wrong place and get a serious cut.
- **Don't overload the dies.** Each die has a maximum number of layers that can be cut. Make sure you know the limits based on the die and machine you are using.
- **Always use the mats that go with your machine.** Cutting without a mat can damage your rollers, and cutting with the wrong mats can damage your die.

Piecing Tips

Quilting seams leave very little room for error – when you're working with ¼", every little bit counts, and even small errors add up over time.

Use the Right Needle and Thread

For piecing, we always recommend 75/11 or 80/12 quilting or topstitch needles. These needles are finer and have sharper points than the universal needles that are commonly used. The holes they create are smaller, meaning you'll pierce your fabric in the right place and increase the accuracy of your stitch.

To go with those needles, choose a 60- or 50-weight, 100% cotton thread. Either of these thread weights is a much finer thread than an all-purpose blend, leading to a narrower and more accurate seam.

Why cotton? Cotton has a very high heat tolerance, which can withstand the pressing that we subject our blocks to. Threads with polyester content can melt at high temperatures, making it unsuitable for piecing (though using it for quilting is perfectly fine.)

Check Your Seam Allowance

Not every ¼" is created equal. Do you know whether you are stitching an accurate ¼" seam? Do you know when to use a scant ¼" vs a full ¼"? These are important to know so that you have the most success in piecing a variety of blocks.

Full ¼" seam allowances are typically used for piecing squares and rectangles. A scant ¼" seam allowance is used for triangles and other bias shapes, to account for rounding errors and variances when sewing.

How do you stitch a scant ¼" seam allowance? It may be just a matter of moving your needle over one or two positions. Before you do that, make sure you know what a true ¼" is for your machine!

If you've never checked to see if you're piecing an accurate ¼" seam or you want to understand scant, there's a link to a tutorial on our Pattern Resources page.

Reduce Your Stitch Length

Most machines come out of the box set to a 2.5mm stitch length. This stitch length is perfect for garment construction and home decor, but is too long for piecing.

When using a 2.5mm stitch length, many quilters find it necessary to back-stitch or lock stitches at the beginning of a seam so their units don't unravel, which creates unnecessary bulk and makes it difficult to orient seams. Instead, reduce your stitch length to 1.5 to 2.0mm, and eliminate the back stitch entirely.

Chain Piece for Efficiency

You can piece two blocks at a time, or even work on two projects at a time, so that you never have to cut threads. Chain piecing simply means that when you finish stitching one unit, you insert the next one and keep sewing.

As you chain piece, stitch a few extra stitches beyond each unit before adding the next one. This extra bit of stitching creates space between your units so they don't unravel when you cut them apart.

This method conserves thread and makes your work more efficient. If you need to remove a set of units to press them or continue assembly, stitch onto a scrap (or onto another unit from a different section) until you are able to remove the desired set of units from the machine.

If you aren't chain piecing yet, try it! It will change the way you quilt forever.

Move Your Iron

It's tempting to have an iron set up right next to you at sewing height, so you never have to get up to press. Add in a rolling chair, and walking becomes nearly obsolete! However, getting up to press your units is an opportunity for you to take a break from being in one position, helps with circulation, and reduces stiffness.

Take breaks to stretch too; it is fun to piece for long stretches at a time, but it's really hard on the body.

Press, Clip and Swirl

We use what we consider to be a unique approach to pressing units and blocks, which we will detail here. Our goal is to obtain flat, square blocks, and we will use every method we can to achieve this. We don't always press open, or always press to the dark; we press the direction we need to so the block is flat and square.

This may be unfamiliar territory for you, so when possible, we give guidance on pressing seams during the block construction.

What it Means to Press

In quilting, we do not iron; we press.

Pressing fabric involves setting the iron down onto the fabric and picking it up to move it to the next location, instead of sliding it from one place to another as we would do when ironing. Ironing stretches fabric and the last thing you want to do is stretch your units out of shape.

After stitching each seam, press with the iron before opening it to set the seam. This settles your stitches into the fabric. Once your seam is set, open and press as directed.

We recommend an iron set to the highest setting for cotton fabrics, without steam. As previously mentioned, introducing moisture during the piecing process can cause accuracy issues, especially if you haven't prewashed. If you wish to starch your fabrics, do so at the beginning of the project, before you start cutting.

What it Means to Clip

Sometimes, we will have a unit with a seam pressed in one direction, but to attach it to a subsequent unit, we may need to twist the seam allowance. To prevent this twist from distorting the block, we use a pair of small, sharp scissors to clip into the seam and release the twist in the fabric.

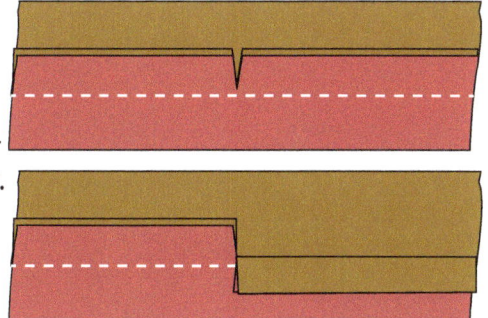

When clipping, don't clip the stitches themselves or beyond so you don't create a hole in your quilt.

We also recommend that you reduce your stitch length (between 1.5 to 2.0mm) so that your seams are stronger and able to withstand a clipped seam.

What it Means to Swirl

When multiple fabrics come together at an intersection, the best way to distribute bulk is to swirl the seams. This is a common technique for four- and nine-patches, but you'd be surprised by how you can apply this technique to just about any block with intersections. Swirling a seam properly requires planning ahead a bit when pressing seams, but if a seam isn't facing the right direction, you can always clip it to do the swirl.

To swirl a seam, work your way around the unit, pressing seams in a clockwise (or counter clockwise) direction. At the center, use your fingers to open up the seams so they also are pressed in the same direction.

You may need to use a seam ripper to remove 1–2 stitches at the center to allow it to open flat. Press the center from the back, then turn your block over and press it again from the front.

Using Specialty Rulers

There are so many ways to use tools, rulers, templates and techniques to achieve accurate shapes for quilting. For this pattern, you may decide to use other methods, but we don't want you to be confused by the options.

The pattern assumes that you will either use regular rotary or die cutting to make the quilt, but if you choose to use one of the optional specialty rulers we recommended for this pattern, you can substitute the cutting instructions in the following chart.

These rulers may require a different number of strips than the pattern specifies. Start with fewer strips than the pattern states, and cut additional strips as needed to finish the block.

Finished Size	*Regular Rotary Cutting* — *Follow the pattern*	*A Little Nervous About Accuracy?* — *Cut this size instead*	*Using a Specialty Ruler?* — *Cut this size instead*	*Are You Die Cutting?* — *Use the EDeN™ Chart*
2" finished HST	Cut 2⅞" strips	Cut 3" strips into 3" squares. Cut along one diagonal. Square up to 2½" after sewing.	Cut strips 2½"; follow tool instructions on packaging	HST-2
3" finished HST	Cut 3⅞" strips	Cut 4" strips into 4" squares. Cut along one diagonal. Square up to 3½" after sewing.	Cut strips 3½"; follow tool instructions on packaging	HST-3
4" finished QST	Cut 5¼" strips	Cut 5½" strips into 5½" squares. Cut along both diagonals. Square up to 4½" after sewing.	Cut strips 2½"; follow tool instructions on packaging	QST-4
6" finished HST	Cut 6⅞" strips	Cut 7" strips into 7" squares. Cut along one diagonal. Square up to 6½" after sewing.	Cut strips 6½"; follow tool instructions on packaging	HST-6
6" finished QST	Cut 7¼" strips	Cut 7½" strips into 7½" squares. Cut along both diagonals. Square up to 6½" after sewing.	Cut strips 3½"; follow tool instructions on packaging	QST-6
8" finished QST	Cut 9¼" strips	Cut 9½" strips into 9½" squares. Cut along both diagonals. Square up to 8½" after sewing.	Cut strips 4½"; follow tool instructions on packaging	QST-8

Month 1: Starfish & Churn Dash

Block 1A
Make 1
Finished: 12" × 12"
Unfinished: 12½" × 12½"

Block 1B
Make 1
Finished: 12" × 12"
Unfinished: 12½" × 12½"

Block 1C
Make 6
Finished: 6" × 6"
Unfinished: 6½" × 6½"

Cutting:

Fabric #	Fabric Swatch	Reference Illustration	Instructions

7	 311903551	 Turquoise	o Cut (1) 2⅞" × WOF strip.
			  o From strip, cut (12) 2⅞" squares. Cut along one diagonal to make (24) Fabric 7 HSTs. [HST-2]
			o Cut (1) 1½" × WOF Fabric 7 strip. [STR-1]
			o Cut (1) 2½" × WOF strip.
			  o Cut in half widthwise to make (2) 2½" × 20" strips.
			    o From one 2½" × 20" strip, cut (6) 2½" Fabric 7 squares. [SQ-2]
			    o From remaining 2½" × 20" strip, cut (1) 1½" × 20" Fabric 7 strip. [STR-1]

8	 311903849	 Mulberry	o Cut (1) 3⅜" × WOF strip.
			  o From strip, cut (5) 3⅜" Fabric 8 squares. [SOP-4]
			    o From remaining 3⅜" × 23" strip, cut (1) 2⅞" × 23" strip.
			      o From strip, cut (4) 2⅞" squares. Cut along one diagonal to make (8) Fabric 8 HSTs. [HST-2]

more cutting ahead...

Fabric #	Fabric Swatch	Reference Illustration	Instructions

10	 311904100	Light Aqua	o Cut (1) 4¾" × WOF strip.
			  o Cut strip in half widthwise to make (2) 4¾" × 20" strips.
			    o From one 4¾" × 20" strip, cut (1) 2⅞" × 20" strip.
			      o From strip, cut (4) 2⅞" squares. Cut along one diagonal to make (8) Fabric 10 HSTs. [HST-2]
			    o Set aside remaining 4¾" × 20" strip to use in Month 4.

12	 311905065	Orange	o Cut (1) 3⅜" × WOF strip.
			  o From strip, cut (5) 3⅜" Fabric 12 squares. [SOP-4]
			    o From remaining 3⅜" × 23" strip, cut (1) 2⅞" × 23" strip.
			      o From strip, cut (4) 2⅞" squares. Cut along one diagonal to make (8) Fabric 12 HSTs. [HST-2]

15	SPRINKLES	Neutral	o Cut (1) 9¼" × WOF strip.
			  o From strip, cut (2) 9¼" squares. Cut along both diagonals to make (8) Fabric 15 QSTs. [QST-8]
			    o Set aside remaining 9¼" × 21" strip to use in Month 5.
			o Cut (2) 2⅞" × WOF strips.
			  o From strips, cut (20) 2⅞" squares. Cut along one diagonal to make (40) Fabric 15 HSTs. [HST-2]
			    o Set aside remaining 2⅞" × 16" strip to use in Month 5.
			o Cut (2) 1½" × WOF strips.
			  o Cut one strip in half widthwise to make (2) 1½" × 20" Fabric 15 strips. [STR-1]
			    o Set aside one 1½" × 20" strip as scrap.

Making Block 1A:

1. Sew the short side of (1) Fabric 12 HST to the short side of (1) Fabric 10 HST. Press the seam toward the Fabric 12 HST.

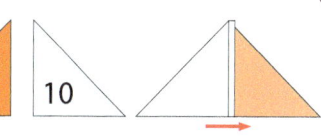

2. Sew the short side of (1) Fabric 12 HST to the short side of (1) Fabric 15 HST. Press the seam toward the Fabric 12 HST.

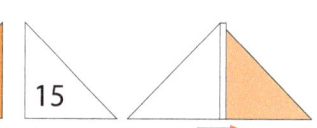

 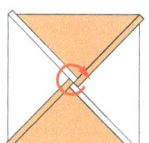 

Make 4

3. Nest the seams and sew the 12/10 triangle to the 12/15 triangle. Swirl the seam allowances to make a 3⅜" × 3⅜" hourglass square. Make 4.

4. Sew (1) hourglass square to (1) 3⅜" × 3⅜" Fabric 8 square, noting the orientation of the hourglass square. Press the seam toward the Fabric 8 square to make a 3⅜" × 6¼" Unit A. Make 4.

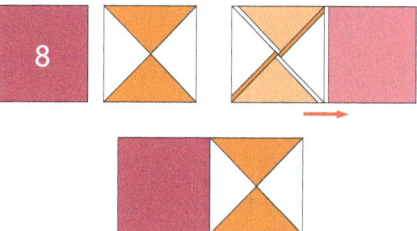

Unit A - Make 4

5. Sew a Unit A between (2) Fabric 15 QSTs as shown. Press the seams toward the Fabric 15 QSTs to make a Unit B. Make 2.

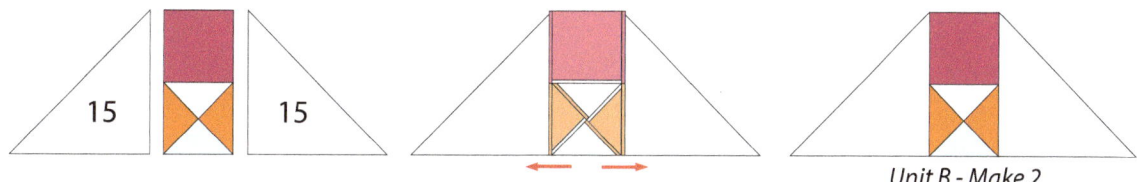

Unit B - Make 2

6. Sew (1) Fabric 8 square between (2) Unit As, noting the orientation of the units. Press the seams toward the center square to make a 3⅜" × 14⅞" Unit C.

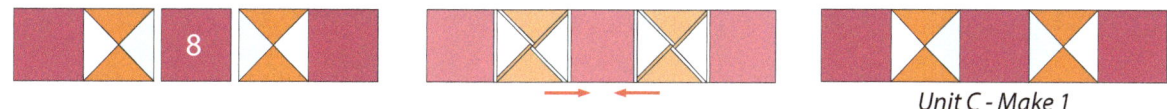

Unit C - Make 1

7. Sew the Unit C between the (2) Unit Bs, noting the orientation of each unit. Clip and swirl seam allowance as needed and press flat.

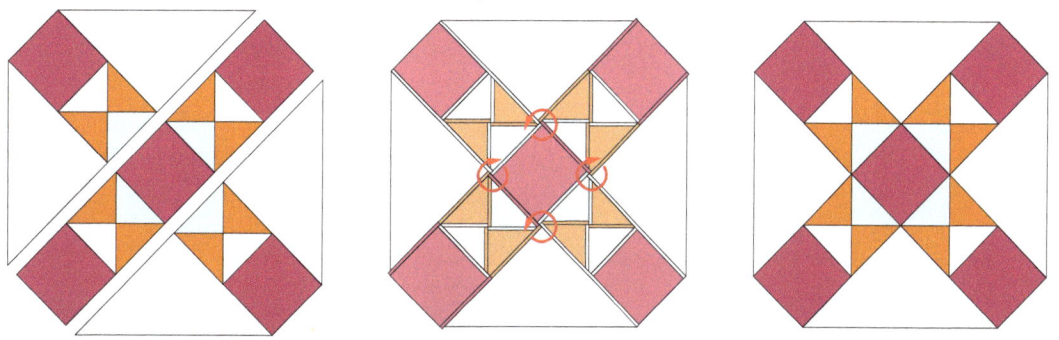

Month 1: Starfish & Churn Dash

8. Sew a Fabric 15 HST to each of the (4) Fabric 8 corners. Press the seams toward the Fabric 15 corners to make a 12½" × 12½" Block 1A.

 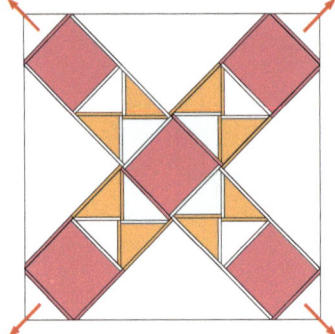 

Block 1A - Make 1

Making Block 1B:

1. Sew the short side of (1) Fabric 8 HST to the short side of (1) Fabric 10 HST. Press the seam toward the Fabric 8 HST.

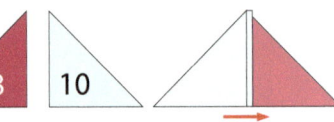

2. Sew the short side of (1) Fabric 8 HST to the short side of (1) Fabric 15 HST. Press the seam toward the Fabric 8 HST.

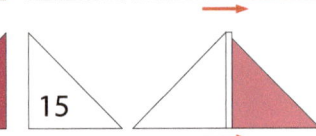

Make 4

3. Nest the seams and sew the 8/10 triangle to the 8/15 triangle. Swirl the seam allowances to make a 3⅜" × 3⅜" hourglass square. Make 4.

4. Sew (1) hourglass square to (1) 3⅜" × 3⅜" Fabric 12 square, noting the orientation of the hourglass square. Press the seam toward the Fabric 12 square to make a 3⅜" × 6¼" Unit A. Make 4.

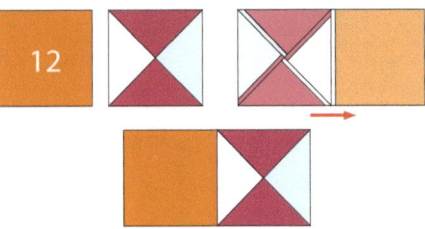

Unit A - Make 4

5. Sew a Unit A between (2) Fabric 15 QSTs as shown. Press the seams toward the Fabric 15 QSTs to make a Unit B. Make 2.

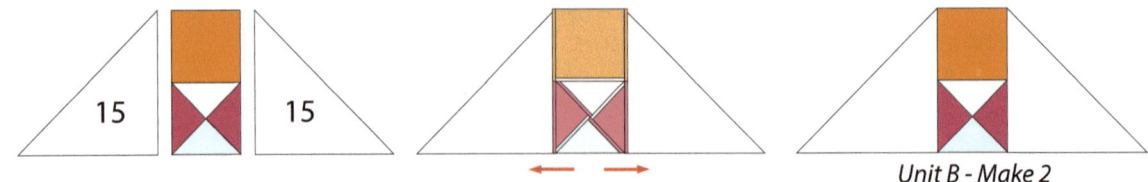

Unit B - Make 2

6. Sew (1) Fabric 12 square between (2) Unit As, noting the orientation of the units. Press the seams toward the center square to make a 3⅜" × 14⅞" Unit C.

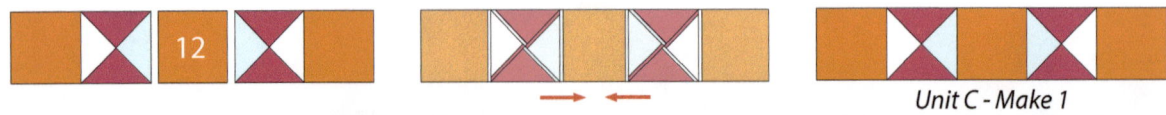

Unit C - Make 1

7. Sew the Unit C between the (2) Unit Bs, noting the orientation of each unit. Clip and swirl seam allowance as needed and press flat.

 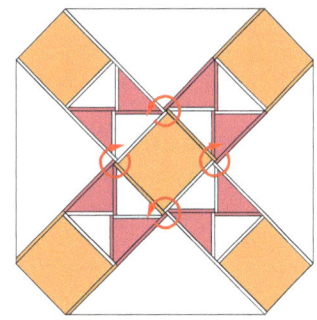 

8. Sew a Fabric 15 HST to each of the (4) Fabric 12 corners. Press the seams toward the Fabric 15 corners to make a 12½" × 12½" Block 1B.

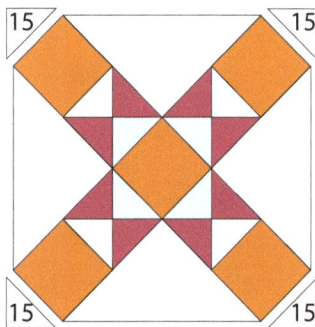 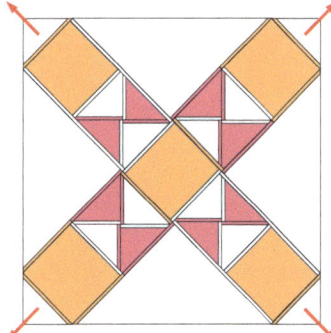 

Block 1B - Make 1

Making Block 1C:

1. Sew (1) 1½" × WOF Fabric 7 strip to (1) 1½" × WOF Fabric 15 strip. Press the seam open to make a 2½" × WOF long two-strip panel.

2. Sew (1) 1½" × 20" Fabric 7 strip to (1) 1½" × 20" Fabric 15 strip. Press the seam open to make a 2½" × 20" short two-strip panel.

3. Crosscut the panels into 2½" sections for a total of (24) 2½" × 2½" side squares.

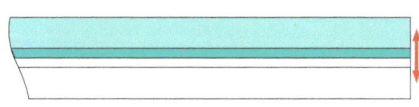 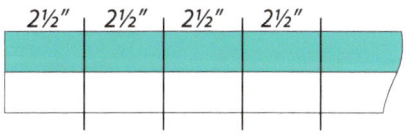 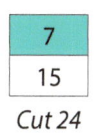

Cut 24

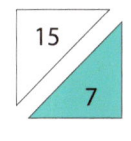 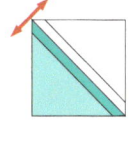 

Make 24

4. Sew (1) Fabric 7 HST to (1) Fabric 15 HST as shown. Press the seam open to make a 2½" × 2½" corner square. Make 24.

5. Lay out (4) side squares, (4) corner squares and (1) 2½" × 2½" Fabric 7 square in three rows of three squares each, noting the placement and orientation of each square.

6. Sew the squares together in each row. Press the seams toward the side squares to make a 2½" × 6½" row.

Month 1: Starfish & Churn Dash

7. Join the rows, nesting the seams. Clip and swirl the seams and press flat to make a 6½" × 6½" Block 1C. Make 6 blocks.

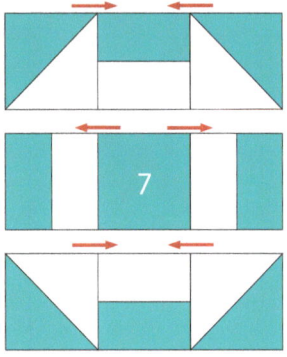 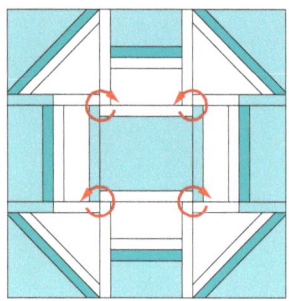 

Block 1C - Make 6

Month 2: Friendship Stars & Churn Dash

Block 2A
Make 5
Finished: 6" × 6"
Unfinished: 6½" × 6½"

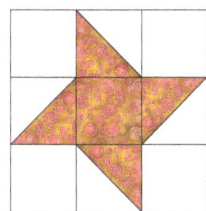

Block 2B
Make 4
Finished: 6" × 6"
Unfinished: 6½" × 6½"

Block 2C
Make 9
Finished: 6" × 6"
Unfinished: 6½" × 6½"

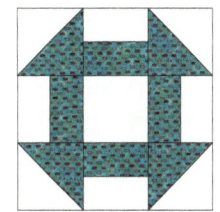

Cutting:

Fabric #	Fabric Swatch	Reference Illustration	Instructions
1	 311901340	 Burgundy	o Cut (1) 2⅞" × WOF strip. 　o From strip, cut (8) 2⅞" squares. Cut along one diagonal to make (16) Fabric 1 HSTs. [HST-2] 　　o From remaining 2⅞" × 16" strip, cut (1) 2½" × 16" strip. 　　　o From strip, cut (4) 2½" Fabric 1 squares. [SQ-2]
4	 311902610	 Dark Teal	o Cut (1) 2⅞" × WOF strip. 　o From strip, cut (13) 2⅞" squares. Cut along one diagonal to make (26) Fabric 4 HSTs. [HST-2] o Cut (1) 7¼" × WOF strip. 　o Cut strip in half widthwise to make (2) 7¼" × 20" strips. 　　o From one 7¼" × 20" strip, cut (1) 2⅞" × 20" strip. 　　　o From strip, cut (5) 2⅞" squares. Cut along one diagonal to make (10) Fabric 4 HSTs. [HST-2] o Set aside remaining 7¼" × 20" strip to use in Month 5. o Cut (3) 1½" × WOF strips. 　o Cut (1) strip in half widthwise to make (2) 1½" × 20" Fabric 4 strips. [STR-1] 　　o Set aside (1) 1½" × 20" strip as scrap.

more cutting ahead...

Fabric #	Fabric Swatch	Reference Illustration	Instructions

12	311905065	Orange	o Cut (1) 2⅞" × WOF strip.
			  o From strip, cut (10) 2⅞" squares. Cut along one diagonal to make (20) Fabric 12 HSTs. [HST-2]
			o Cut (1) 2½" × WOF strip.
			  o From strip, cut (5) 2½" Fabric 12 squares. [SQ-2]

15	SPRINKLES	Neutral	o Cut (3) 2⅞" × WOF strips.
			  o From strips, cut (36) 2⅞" squares. Cut along one diagonal to make (72) Fabric 15 HSTs. [HST-2]
			o Cut (3) 1½" × WOF strips.
			  o Cut (1) strip in half widthwise to make (2) 1½" × 20" Fabric 15 strips. [STR-1]
			    o Set aside one 1½" × 20" strip to use in Month 5.
			o Cut (3) 2½" × WOF strips.
			  o From strips, cut (45) 2½" Fabric 15 squares. [SQ-2]

Stardust

Making Block 2A:

1. Sew (1) Fabric 12 HST to (1) Fabric 15 HST as shown. Press the seam open to make a 2½" × 2½" side square. Make 20.

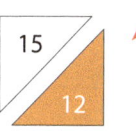 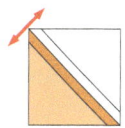 

Make 20

2. Lay out (4) side squares, (4) 2½" × 2½" Fabric 15 squares and (1) 2½" × 2½" Fabric 12 square in three rows of three squares each, noting the placement and orientation of each side square.

3. Sew the squares together in each row. Press the seams toward the solid squares to make a 2½" × 6½" row.

4. Join the rows, nesting the seams. Swirl the seams and press flat to make a 6½" × 6½" Block 2A. Make 5 blocks.

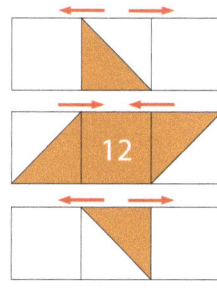 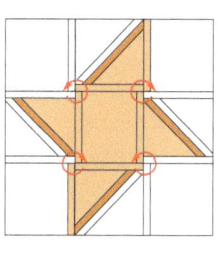 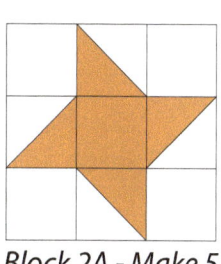

Block 2A - Make 5

Making Block 2B:

1. Sew (1) Fabric 1 HST to (1) Fabric 15 HST as shown. Press the seam open to make a 2½" × 2½" side square. Make 16.

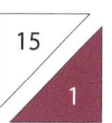 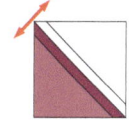 

Make 16

2. Lay out (4) side squares, (4) 2½" × 2½" Fabric 15 squares and (1) 2½" × 2½" Fabric 1 square in three rows of three squares each, noting the placement and orientation of each side square.

3. Sew the squares together in each row. Press the seams toward the solid squares to make a 2½" × 6½" row.

4. Join the rows, nesting the seams. Swirl the seams and press flat to make a 6½" × 6½" Block 2B. Make 4 blocks.

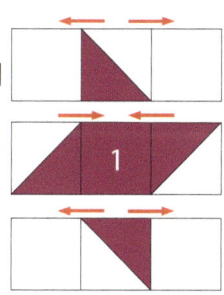 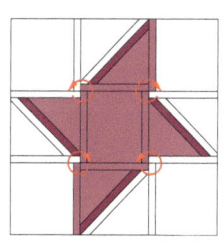 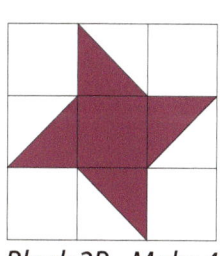

Block 2B - Make 4

Making Block 2C:

1. Sew (1) 1½" × WOF Fabric 4 strip to (1) 1½" × WOF Fabric 15 strip. Press the seam open to make a 2½" × WOF long two-strip panel. Make 2 long two-strip panels.

2. Sew (1) 1½" × 20" Fabric 4 strip to (1) 1½" × 20" Fabric 15 strip. Press the seam open to make a 2½" × 20" short two-strip panel.

Month 2: Friendship Stars & Churn Dash

3. Crosscut the panels into 2½" sections for a total of (36) 2½" × 2½" side squares.

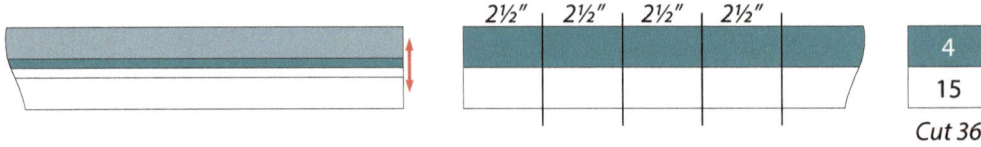

Cut 36

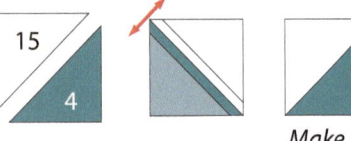

Make 36

4. Sew (1) Fabric 4 HST to (1) Fabric 15 HST as shown. Press the seam open to make a 2½" × 2½" corner square. Make 36.

5. Lay out (4) side squares, (4) corner squares and (1) 2½" × 2½" Fabric 15 square in three rows of three squares each, noting the placement and orientation of each square.

6. Sew the squares together in each row. Press the seams toward the side squares to make a 2½" × 6½" row.

7. Join the rows, nesting the seams. Swirl the seams and press flat to make a 6½" × 6½" Block 2C. Make 9 blocks.

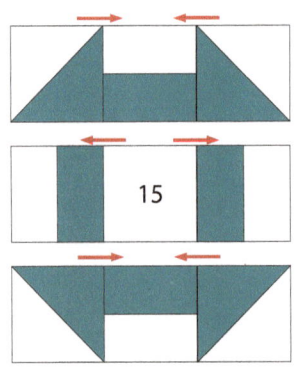 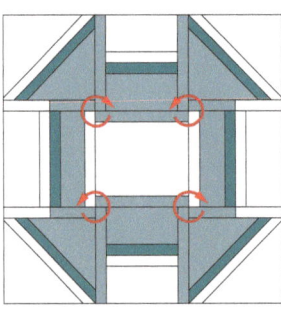 

Block 2C - Make 9

Month 3: Ohio Star & Flying Geese

Block 3A
Make 1
Finished: 12" × 12"
Unfinished: 12½" × 12½"

Block 3B
Make 10
Finished: 6" × 6"
Unfinished: 6½" × 6½"

Block 3C
Make 10
Finished: 6" × 6"
Unfinished: 6½" × 6½"

Cutting:

Fabric #	Fabric Swatch	Reference Illustration	Instructions

3	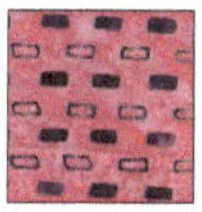 311902360	 Pink	o Cut (1) 7¼" × WOF strip.
			  o From strip, cut (3) 7¼" squares. Cut along both diagonals to make (12) Fabric 3 QSTs. [QST-6]
			    o Set aside (2) QSTs as scrap.

5	 311902851	 Violet	o Cut (1) 7¼" × WOF strip.
			  o From strip, cut (3) 7¼" squares. Cut along both diagonals to make (12) Fabric 5 QSTs. [QST-6]
			    o Set aside (2) QSTs as scrap.

6	 311903060	 Gold	o Cut (1) 7¼" × WOF strip.
			  o From strip, cut (3) 7¼" squares. Cut along both diagonals to make (12) Fabric 6 QSTs. [QST-6]
			    o Set aside (2) QSTs as scrap.
			  o From remaining 7¼" × 18" strip, cut (1) 4½" Fabric 6 square. [SQ-4]

11	 311904502	 Med. Aqua	o Cut (1) 7¼" × WOF strip.
			  o From strip, cut (1) 7¼" × 28" strip and (1) 7¼" × 12" strip.
			    o From 7¼" × 12" strip, cut (1) 5¼" × 12" strip.
			      o From strip, cut (2) 5¼" squares. Cut along both diagonals to make (8) Fabric 11 QSTs. [QST-4]
			  o Set aside 7¼" × 28" strip to use in Month 5.

more cutting ahead...

Fabric #	Fabric Swatch	Reference Illustration	Instructions

13	311905330	Fuchsia	o Cut (1) 7¼" × WOF strip.
			  o From strip, cut (3) 7¼" squares. Cut along both diagonals to make (12) Fabric 13 QSTs. [QST-6]
			  o Set aside (2) QSTs as scrap.

14	311905585	Navy	o Cut (1) 5¼" × WOF strip.
			  o From strip, cut (1) 5¼" square. Cut along both diagonals to make (4) Fabric 14 QSTs. [QST-4]
			  o Set aside remaining 5¼" × 34" strip to use in Month 5.

15	SPRINKLES	Neutral	o Cut (4) 3⅞" × WOF strips.
			  o From strips, cut (40) 3⅞" squares. Cut along one diagonal to make (80) Fabric 15 HSTs. [HST-3]
			o Cut (1) 5¼" × WOF strip.
			  o From strip, cut (1) 5¼" square. Cut along both diagonals to make (4) Fabric 15 QSTs. [QST-4]
			  o From remaining 5¼" × 34" strip, cut (1) 4½" × 34" strip.
			    o From strip, cut (4) 4½" Fabric 15 squares. [SQ-4]

Making Block 3A:

1. Sew the short side of (1) Fabric 11 QST to the short side of (1) Fabric 14 QST. Press the seam toward the Fabric 11 QST.

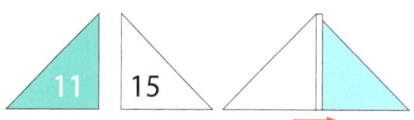

2. Sew the short side of (1) Fabric 11 QST to the short side of (1) Fabric 15 QST. Press the seam toward the Fabric 11 QST.

Make 4

3. Nest the seams and sew the 11/14 triangle to the 11/15 triangle. Swirl the seam allowances to make a 4½" × 4½" hourglass square. Make 4.

4. Lay out (4) hourglass squares, (1) Fabric 6 square, and (4) Fabric 15 squares into three rows of three squares each, noting the placement and orientation of each side square.

5. Sew the squares together in each row. Press the seams toward the solid squares to make a 4½" × 12½" row.

6. Join the rows, nesting the seams. Clip and swirl the seams and press flat to make a 12½" × 12½" Block 3A. Make 1.

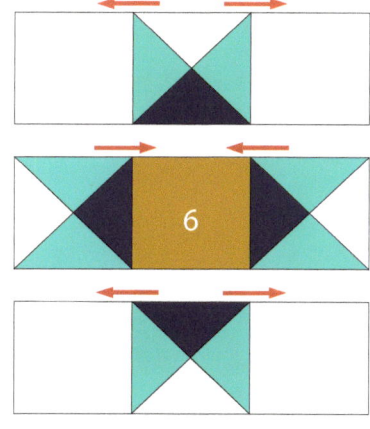 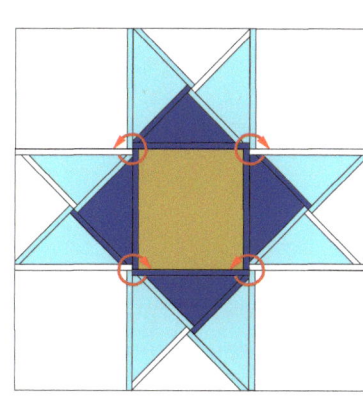 

Block 3A - Make 1

Making Block 3B:

1. Sew the long side of (1) Fabric 15 HST to the right short side of (1) Fabric 13 QST. Press the seam open.

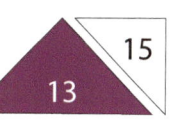 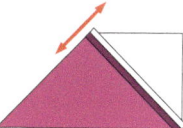

2. Sew another Fabric 15 HST to the left side of the Fabric 13/15 unit. Press the seam open to make a 3½" × 6½" Unit A. Make 10.

 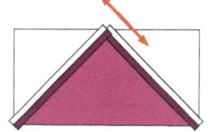 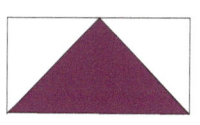

Unit A - Make 10

Month 3: Ohio Star & Flying Geese

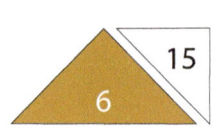 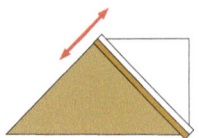

3. Sew the long side of (1) Fabric 15 HST to the right short side of (1) Fabric 6 QST. Press the seam open.

4. Sew another Fabric 15 HST to the left side of the Fabric 6/15 unit. Press the seam open to make a 3½" × 6½" Unit B. Make 10.

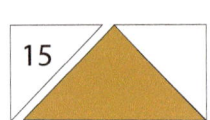 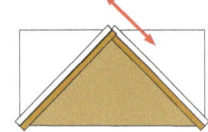 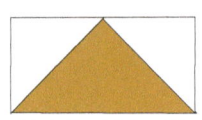

Unit B - Make 10

5. Stitch (1) Unit A to the top of (1) Unit B. Press the seam toward Unit A to make a 6½" × 6½" Block 3B. Make 10.

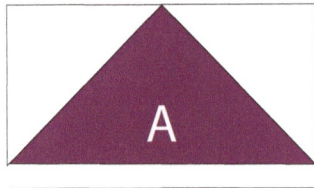
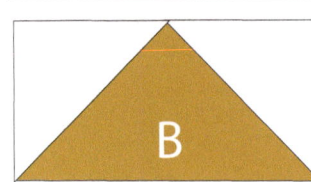

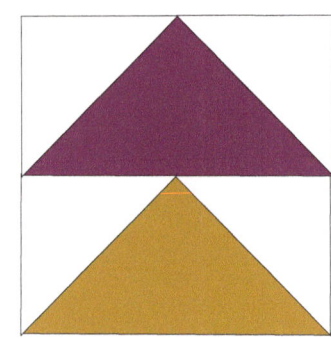

Block 3B - Make 10

Making Block 3C:

1. Sew the long side of (1) Fabric 15 HST to the right short side of (1) Fabric 5 QST. Press the seam open.

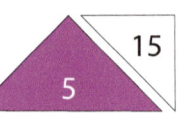 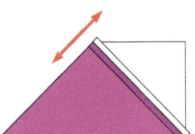

2. Sew another Fabric 15 HST to the left side of the Fabric 5/15 unit. Press the seam open to make a 3½" × 6½" Unit A. Make 10.

 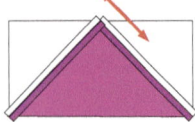 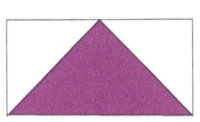

Unit A - Make 10

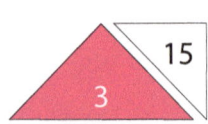 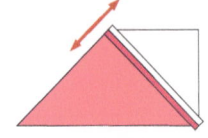

3. Sew the long side of (1) Fabric 15 HST to the right short side of (1) Fabric 3 QST. Press the seam open.

Stardust

4. Sew another Fabric 15 HST to the left side of the Fabric 3/15 unit. Press the seam open to make a 3½" × 6½" Unit B. Make 10.

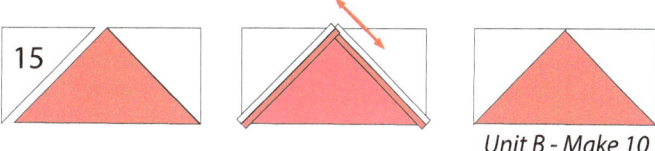

Unit B - Make 10

5. Stitch (1) Unit A to the top of (1) Unit B. Press the seam toward Unit A to make a 6½" × 6½" Block 3C. Make 10.

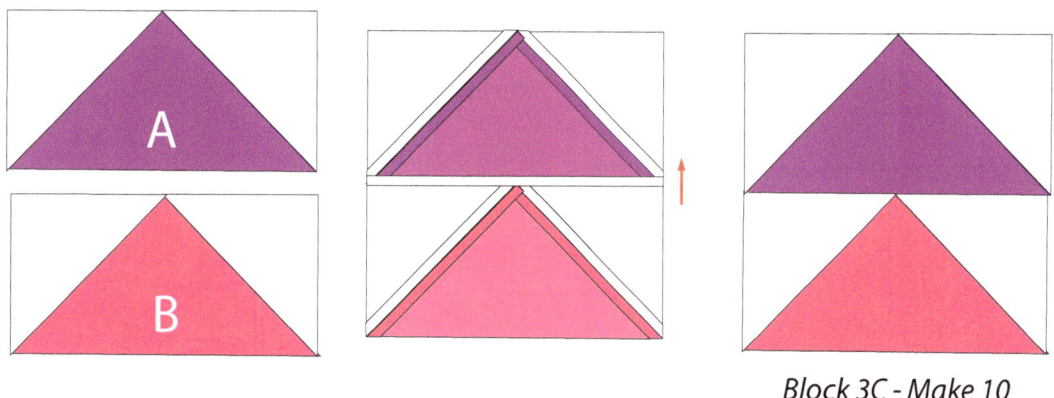

Block 3C - Make 10

Become a Binding Superhero!
beautiful binding finished completely by machine

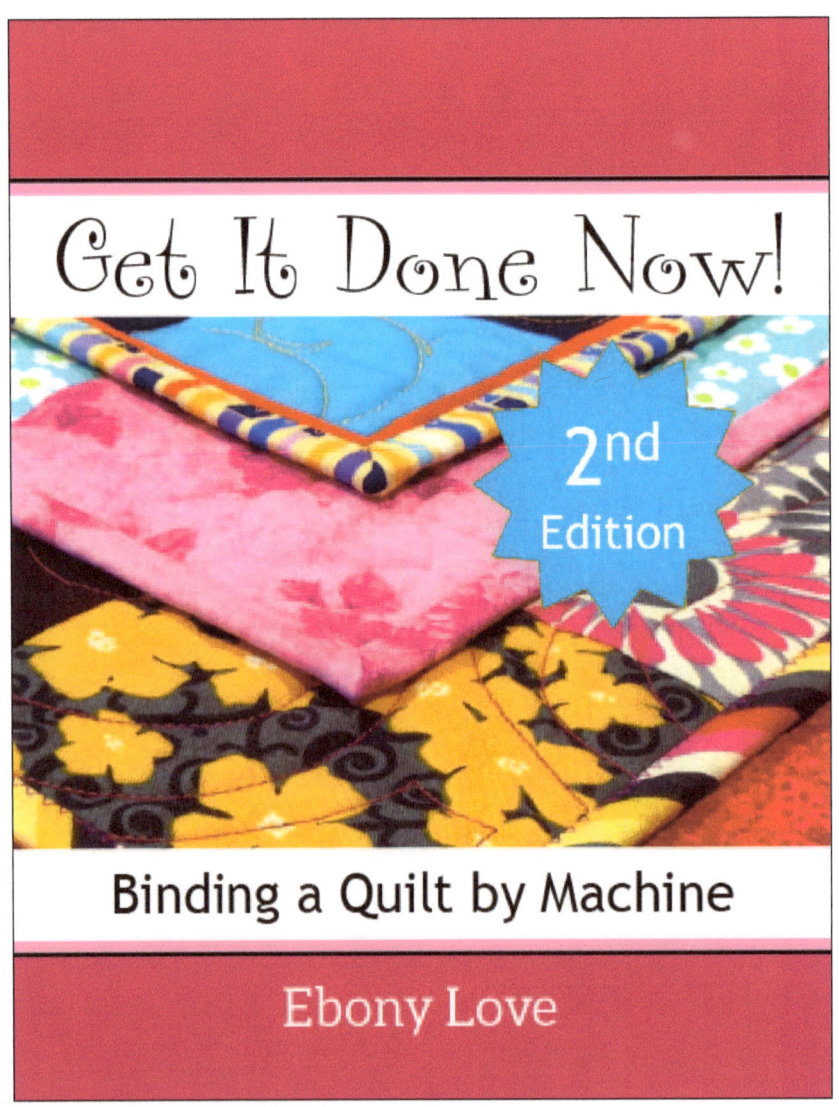

available from your local independent shop or online at bindingbymachine.com

Month 4: Orange Stars

Block 4A
Make 1
Finished: 18" × 18"
Unfinished: 18½" × 18½"

Block 4B
Make 1
Finished: 18" × 18"
Unfinished: 18½" × 18½"

Cutting:

Fabric #	Fabric Swatch	Reference Illustration	Instructions
1	 311901340	Burgundy	o Cut (1) 4¾" × WOF strip. o From strip, cut (5) 4¾" Fabric 1 squares. [SOP-6]

6	 311903060	Gold	o Cut (1) 3⅞" × WOF strip.
			  o From strip, cut (6) 3⅞" squares. Cut along one diagonal to make (12) Fabric 6 HSTs. [HST-3]
			    o Set aside remaining 3⅞" × 16" strip to use in Month 5.

7	 311903551	Turquoise	o Cut (1) 7" × WOF strip.
			  o From strip, cut (8) Fabric 7 arches using the Orange Peel Ruler–A Arch or the Arch template provided.
			o Cut (1) 4¾" × WOF strip.
			  o From strip, cut (1) 4¾" Fabric 7 square. [SOP-6]
			    o From remaining 4¾" × 35" strip, cut (1) 3⅞" × 35" strip.
			      o From strip, cut (4) 3⅞" squares. Cut along one diagonal to make (8) Fabric 7 HSTs. [HST-3]

8	 311903849	Mulberry	o Cut (1) 7" × WOF strip. o From strip, cut (8) Fabric 8 arches using the Orange Peel Ruler–A Arch or the Arch template provided.
9	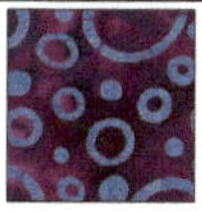 311903885	Dk. Purple	o Cut (2) 4½" × WOF strips. o From strips, cut (8) Fabric 9 melons using the Orange Peel Ruler–B Melon or the Melon template provided.

more cutting ahead...

Fabric #	Fabric Swatch	Reference Illustration	Instructions
10	 311904100	Light Aqua	o From the 4¾" × 20" strip set aside in Month 1, cut (4) 4¾" Fabric 10 squares. [SOP-6]

13	 311905330	Fuchsia	o Cut (1) 3⅞" × WOF strip.
			    o From strip, cut (4) 3⅞" squares. Cut along one diagonal to make (8) Fabric 13 HSTs. [HST-3]
			        o Set aside remaining 3⅞" × 24" strip to use in Month 5.

15	SPRINKLES	Neutral	o Cut (1) 3⅞" × WOF strip. o From strip, cut (6) 3⅞" squares. Cut along one diagonal to make (12) Fabric 15 HSTs. [HST-3]

Making Block 4A:

1. Fold (1) Fabric 9 melon and (2) Fabric 7 arches in half and mark the center of each.

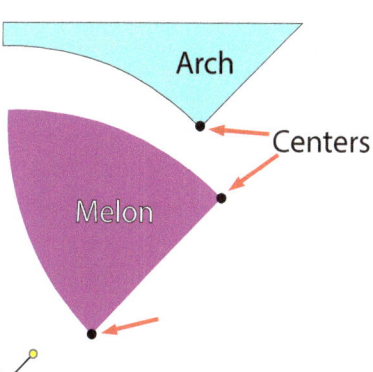

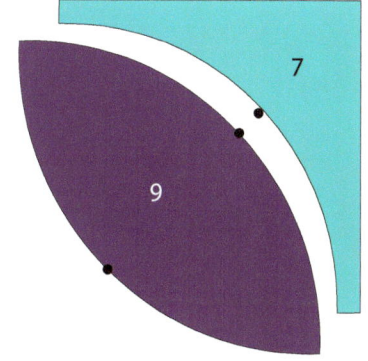
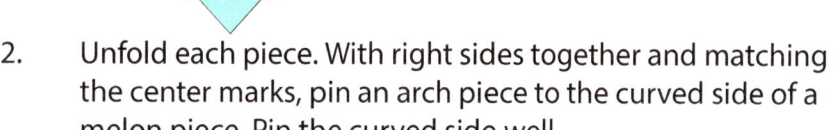

2. Unfold each piece. With right sides together and matching the center marks, pin an arch piece to the curved side of a melon piece. Pin the curved side well.

3. Sew, using a scant ¼" seam allowance along the curve. Press seam toward the Fabric 7 arch.

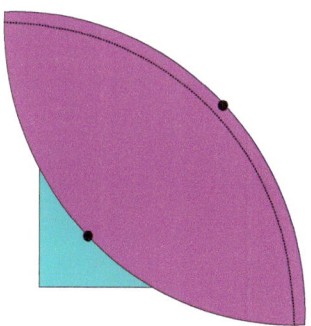 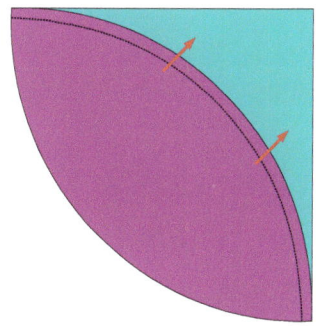 

4. With right sides together and matching the center marks, pin a second arch piece to the remaining curved side of the melon piece. Pin the curved side well.

5. Sew, using a scant ¼" seam allowance along the curve. Press seam toward the Fabric 7 arch to make a 6½" × 6½" Unit A. Make 4.

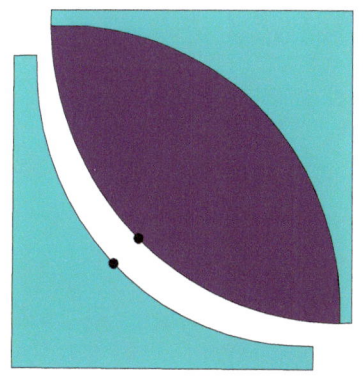 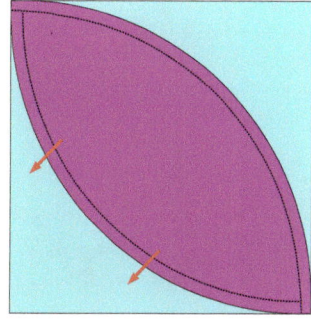 

Unit A - Make 4

6. Sew the long side of (2) Fabric 13 HSTs to the adjacent sides of (1) 4¾" Fabric 10 square. Press the seams open after each HST is sewn.

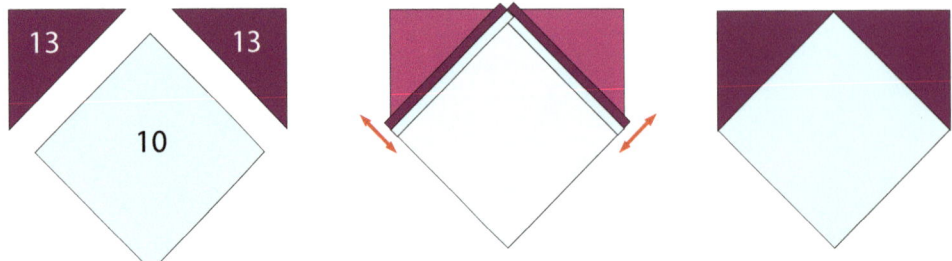

7. Sew the long side of (2) Fabric 6 HSTs to the remaining sides of the Fabric 10 square. Press the seams open after each HST is sewn to make a 6½" × 6½" Unit B. Make 4.

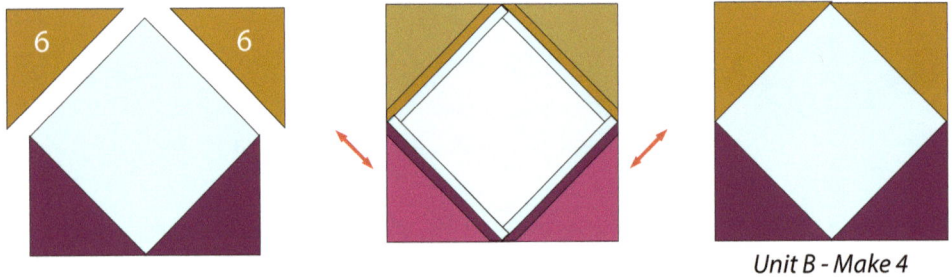

Unit B - Make 4

8. Sew the long side of (2) Fabric 15 HSTs to the adjacent sides of (1) 4¾" Fabric 1 square. Press the seams open after each HST is sewn.

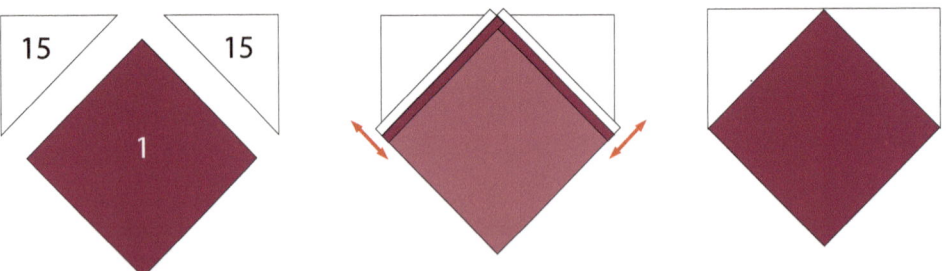

9. Sew the long side of (2) more Fabric 15 HSTs to the remaining sides of the Fabric 1 square. Press the seams open after each HST is sewn to make a 6½" × 6½" Unit C. Make 1.

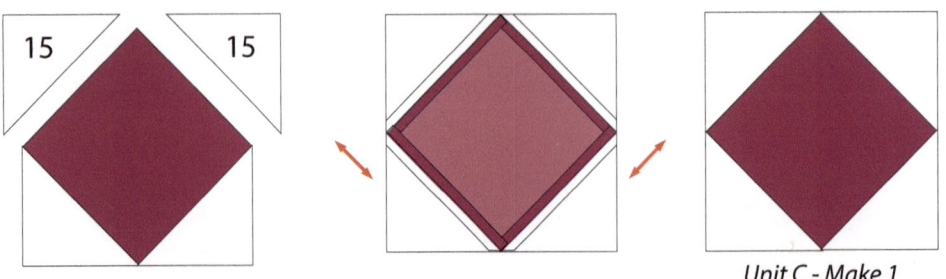

Unit C - Make 1

10. Lay out (4) Unit A squares, (1) Unit C square, and (4) Unit B squares into three rows of three squares each, noting the placement and orientation of each square.

11. Sew the squares together in each row. Press the seams toward the Unit B squares to make a 6½" × 18½" row.

12. Join the rows, nesting the seams. Clip and swirl the seams and press flat to make an 18½" × 18½" Block 4A.

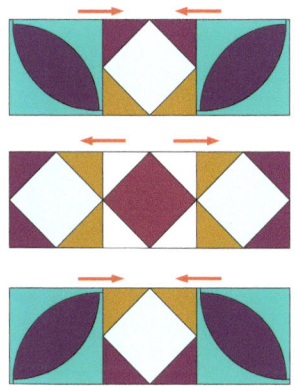  

Block 4A - Make 1

Making Block 4B:

1. Fold (1) Fabric 9 melon and (2) Fabric 8 arches in half and mark the center of each.

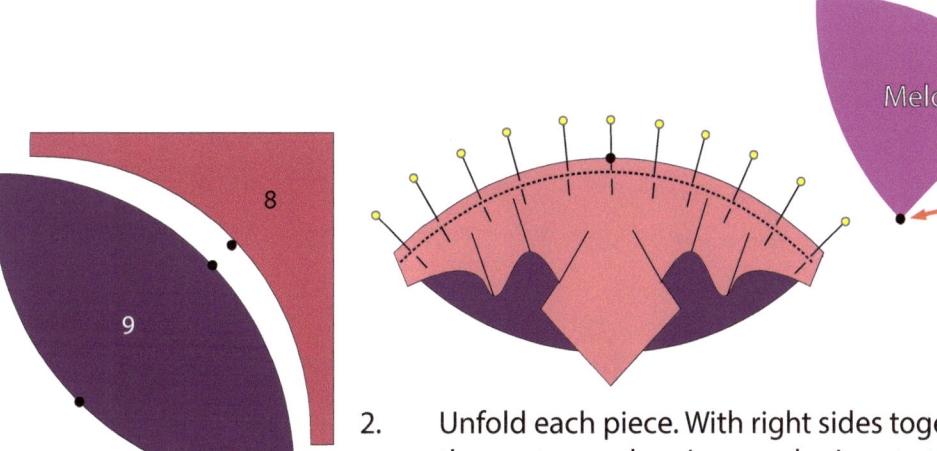

2. Unfold each piece. With right sides together and matching the center marks, pin an arch piece to the curved side of a melon piece. Pin the curved side well.

3. Sew, using a scant ¼" seam allowance along the curve. Press seam toward the Fabric 8 arch.

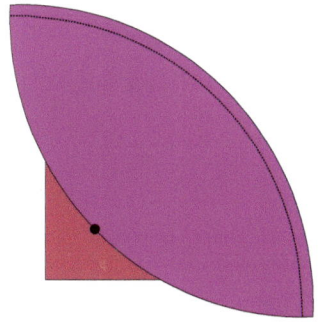 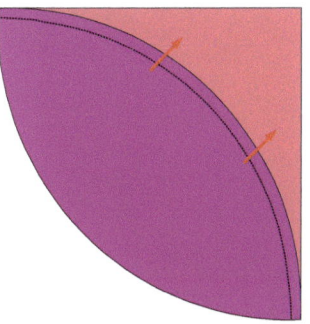 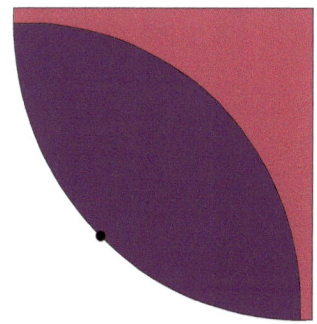

Month 4: Orange Stars

4. With right sides together and matching the center marks, pin a second arch piece to the remaining curved side of the melon piece. Pin the curved side well.

5. Sew, using a scant ¼" seam allowance along the curve. Press seam toward the Fabric 8 arch to make a 6½" × 6½" Unit A. Make 4.

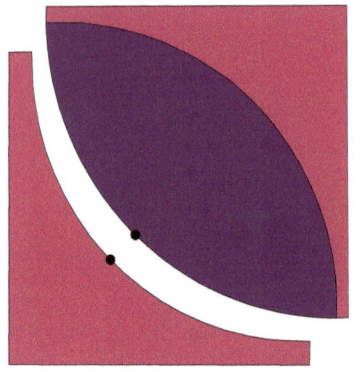 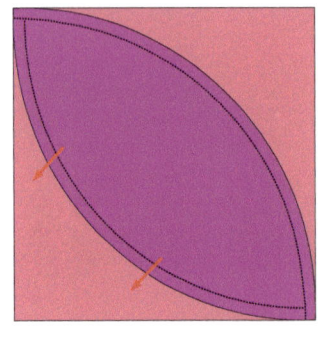 

Unit A - Make 4

6. Sew the long side of (2) Fabric 7 HSTs to the adjacent sides of (1) 4¾" Fabric 1 square. Press the seams open after each HST is sewn.

 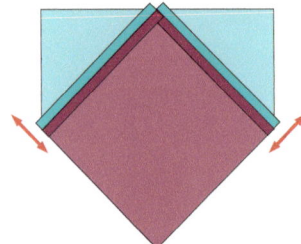 

7. Sew the long side of (2) Fabric 15 HSTs to the remaining sides of the Fabric 1 square. Press the seams open after each HST is sewn to make a 6½" × 6½" Unit B. Make 4.

Unit B - Make 4

8. Sew the long side of (2) Fabric 6 HSTs to the adjacent sides of (1) 4¾" Fabric 7 square. Press the seams open after each HST is sewn.

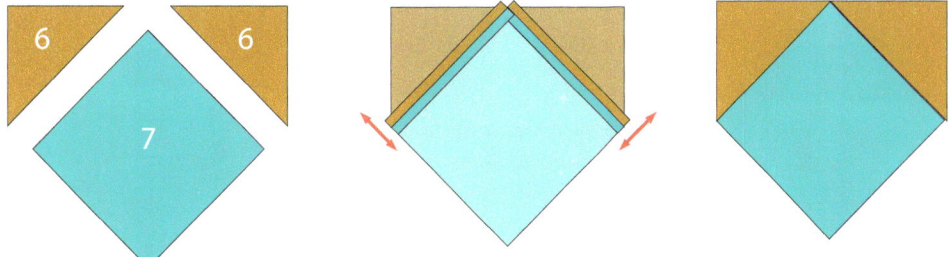

9. Sew the long side of (2) more Fabric 6 HSTs to the remaining sides of the Fabric 7 square. Press the seams open after each HST is sewn to make a 6½" × 6½" Unit C. Make 1.

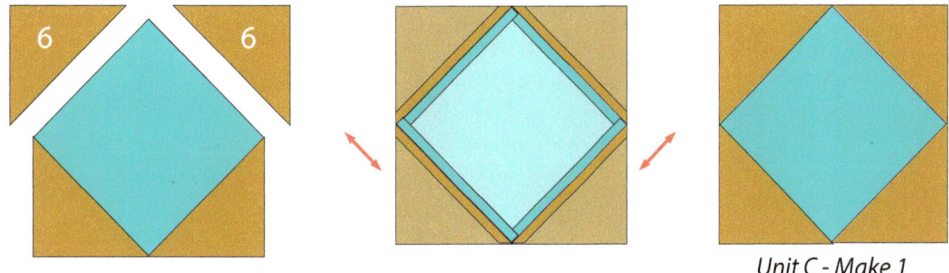

Unit C - Make 1

10. Lay out (4) Unit A squares, (1) Unit C square, and (4) Unit B squares into three rows of three squares each, noting the placement and orientation of each square.

11. Sew the squares together in each row. Press the seams toward the Unit B squares to make a 6½" × 18½" row.

12. Join the rows, nesting the seams. Clip and swirl the seams and press flat to make an 18½" × 18½" Block 4B.

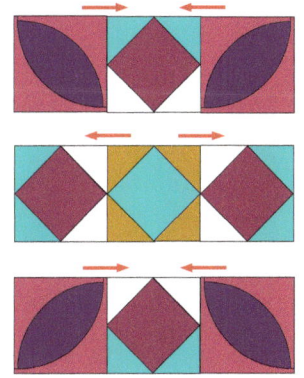  

Block 4B - Make 1

Month 4: Orange Stars

Month 5: Churn Star

Block 5A
Make 1
Finished: 24" × 24"
Unfinished: 24½" × 24½"

Cutting:

Fabric #	Fabric Swatch	Reference Illustration	Instructions

2	311902025	Lt. Cream	o Cut (1) 3⅞" × WOF strip.
			  o From strip, cut (2) 3⅞" squares. Cut along one diagonal to make (4) Fabric 2 HSTs. [HST-3]
			    o Set aside remaining 3⅞" × 32" strip to use in Month 6.

3	311902360	Pink	o Cut (1) 6⅞" × WOF strip. o From strip, cut (4) 6⅞" squares. Cut along one diagonal to make (8) Fabric 3 HSTs. [HST-6]
4	311902610	Dark Teal	o Using 7¼" × 20" strip set aside in Month 2, cut (1) 7¼" square. Cut along both diagonals to make (4) Fabric 4 QSTs. [QST-6]
6	311903060	Gold	o From 3⅞" × 16" strip set aside in Month 4, cut (2) 3⅞" squares. Cut along one diagonal to make (4) Fabric 6 HSTs. [HST-3]
7	311903551	Turquoise	o Cut (1) 3½" × WOF strip. o From strip, cut (4) 3½" Fabric 7 squares. [SQ-3]
9	311903885	Dk. Purple	o Cut (1) 6⅞" × WOF strip. o From strip, cut (2) 6⅞" squares. Cut along one diagonal to make (4) Fabric 9 HSTs. [HST-6]

more cutting ahead...

Fabric #	Fabric Swatch	Reference Illustration	Instructions

11	 311904502	Med. Aqua	o From 7¼" × 28" strip set aside in Month 3, cut (1) 7¼" square. Cut along both diagonals to make (4) Fabric 11 QSTs. [QST-6]
			  o From remaining 7¼" × 20" strip, cut (1) 3⅞" × 20" strip.
			    o From strip, cut (4) 3⅞" squares. Cut along one diagonal to make (8) Fabric 11 HSTs. [HST-3]

13	 311905330	Fuchsia	o From 3⅞" × 24" strip set aside in Month 4, cut (4) 3⅞" squares. Cut along one diagonal to make (8) Fabric 13 HSTs. [HST-3]

14	311905585	Navy	o From 5¼" × 34" strip set aside in Month 3, cut (1) 5¼" × 16" and (1) 5¼" × 7" rectangle.
			  o From 5¼" × 16" rectangle, cut (1) 3⅞" × 16" strip.
			    o From strip, cut (4) 3⅞" squares. Cut along one diagonal to make (8) Fabric 14 HSTs. [HST-3]
			  o From 5¼" × 7" rectangle, cut (1) 2⅞" × 7" strip.
			    o From strip, cut (2) 2⅞" squares. Cut along one diagonal to make (4) Fabric 14 HSTs. [HST-2]
			o Cut (1) 2½" × WOF strip.
			  o From strip, cut (1) 2½" × 11" rectangle and (1) 2½" Fabric 14 square. [SQ-2]
			    o From 2½" × 11" rectangle, cut (1) 1½" × 11" Fabric 14 rectangle. [STR-1]
			o Cut (1) 3½" × WOF strip.
			  o Cut strip in half widthwise to make (2) 3½" × 20" strips.
			    o From one 3½" × 20" strip, cut (4) 3½" Fabric 14 squares. [SQ-3]
			    o Set aside remaining 3½" × 20" strip to use in Month 6.

15	SPRINKLES	Neutral	o From 2⅞" × 16" strip set aside in Month 1, cut (2) 2⅞" squares. Cut along one diagonal to make (4) Fabric 15 HSTs. [HST-2] o From 9¼" × 21" strip set aside in Month 1, cut (1) 7¼" square. Cut along both diagonals to make (4) Fabric 15 QSTs. [QST-6] o From 1½" × 20" strip set aside in Month 2, cut (1) 1½" × 11" Fabric 15 rectangle. [STR-1]

Making Block 5A:

1. Sew the short edge of (1) Fabric 2 HST to the right side of (1) 3½" Fabric 14 square. Press the seam open.

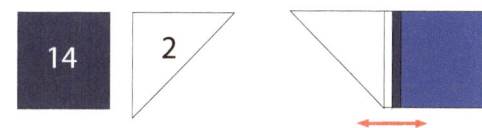

2. Sew the short edge of another Fabric 2 HST to the bottom of the Fabric 2/14 unit to make a pieced HST. Press the seam open.

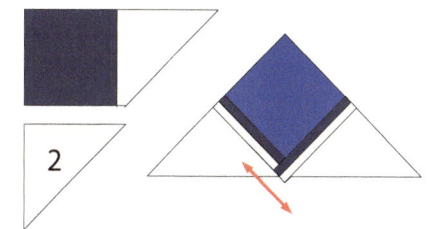

3. Sew the long edge of (1) Fabric 9 HST to the pieced HST unit. Press the seam toward Fabric 9 to make a 6½" × 6½" Unit A. Make 2.

Unit A - Make 2

4. Sew the short edge of (1) Fabric 6 HST to the right side of (1) 3½" Fabric 14 square. Press the seam open.

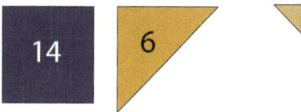

5. Sew the short edge of another Fabric 6 HST to the bottom of the Fabric 6/14 unit to make a pieced HST. Press the seam open.

Month 5: Churn Star

6. Sew the long edge of (1) Fabric 9 HST to the pieced HST unit. Press the seam toward Fabric 9 to make a 6½" × 6½" Unit B. Make 2.

Unit B - Make 2

7. Sew the long side of (1) 3⅞" Fabric 14 HST to the right short side of (1) Fabric 4 QST. Press the seam open.

 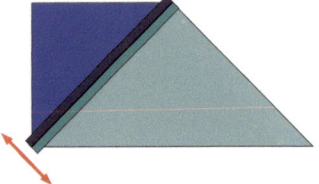

8. Sew another Fabric 14 HST to the left side of the Fabric 4/14 unit. Press the seam open to make a 3½" × 6½" flying geese unit (FG unit). Make 4.

 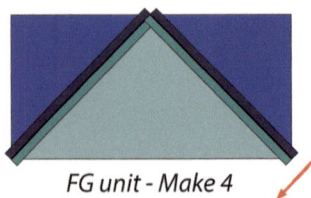

FG unit - Make 4

9. Sew the short edge of (2) Fabric 11 HSTs to the left and right of (1) FG unit. Press the seams open.

10. Sew the long edge of (1) Fabric 11 QST to the top of the FG unit. Press the seam toward the Fabric 11 QST to make a pieced QST geese unit.

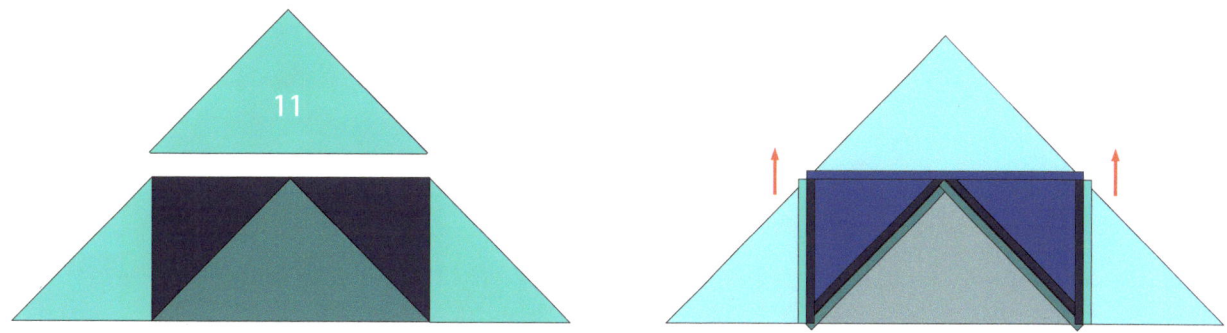

11. Sew the long edge of (1) Fabric 3 HST to the right of the pieced QST geese unit. Press the seam toward the Fabric 3 HST.

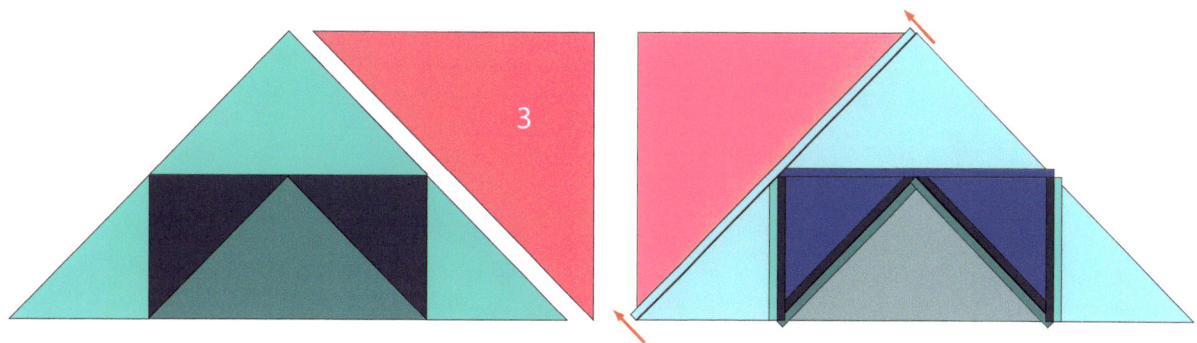

12. Sew the long edge of another Fabric 3 HST to the left of the pieced QST geese unit. Press the seam toward the Fabric 3 HST to make a 6½" × 12½" Unit C. Make 4.

Unit C - Make 4

13. Sew the long side of (1) Fabric 13 HST to the right short side of (1) Fabric 15 QST. Press the seam open.

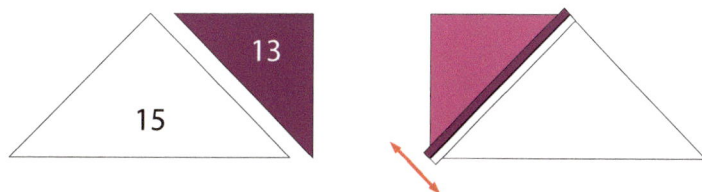

Month 5: Churn Star

14. Sew another Fabric 13 HST to the left side of the Fabric 13/15 unit. Press the seam open to make a 3½" × 6½" Unit D. Make 4.

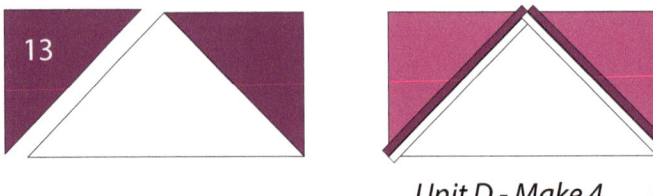

Unit D - Make 4

15. Sew (1) 1½" × 11" Fabric 14 rectangle to (1) 1½" × 11" Fabric 15 rectangle. Press the seam open to make a 2½" × 11" panel.

16. Crosscut the panel into 2½" sections for a total of (4) 2½" × 2½" side squares.

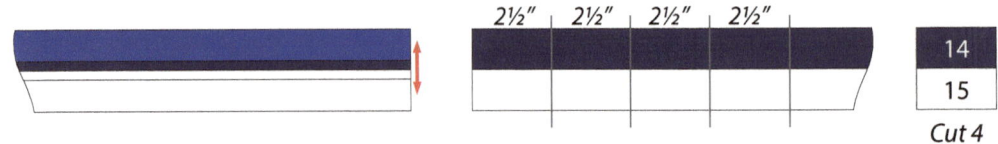

Make 4

17. Sew (1) 2⅞" Fabric 14 HST to (1) 2⅞" Fabric 15 HST as shown. Press the seam open to make a 2½" × 2½" corner square. Make 4.

18. Lay out (4) side squares, (4) corner squares and (1) 2½" × 2½" Fabric 14 square in three rows of three squares each, noting the placement and orientation of each square.

19. Sew the squares together in each row. Press the seams toward the side squares to make a 2½" × 6½" row.

20. Join the rows, nesting the seams. Clip and swirl the seams and press flat to make a 6½" × 6½" Unit E. Make 1 block.

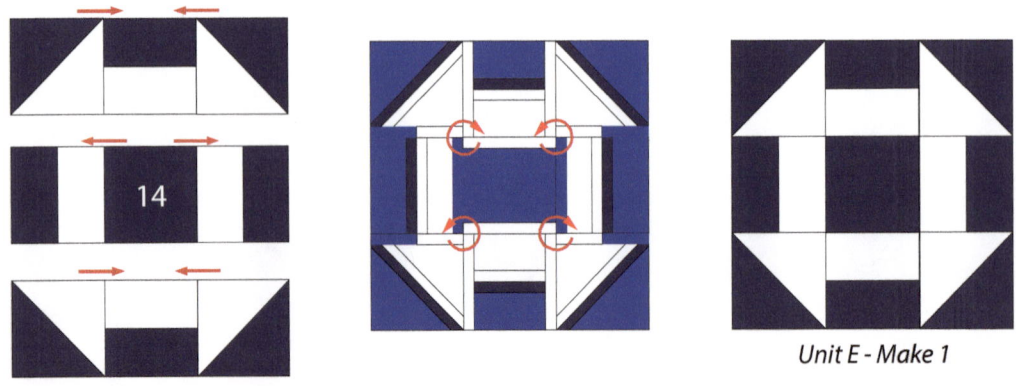

Unit E - Make 1

21. Lay out (1) Unit A, (1) Unit C, and (1) Unit B in a row, noting the placement and orientation of the A and B units. Sew them together. Press the seams away from Unit C to make a 6½" × 24½" A/C/B unit. Make 2.

Unit A/C/B - Make 2

22. Stitch (1) Fabric 7 square to the left of (1) Unit D. Press the seam toward the Fabric 7 square.

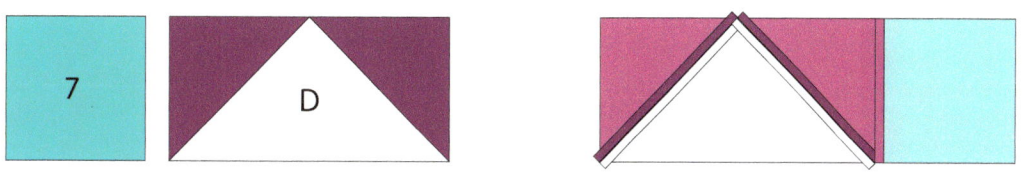

23. Stitch another Fabric 7 square to the right of (1) Unit D. Press the seam toward the Fabric 7 square to make a 3½" × 12½" frame unit. Make 2.

Frame unit - Make 2

Month 5: Churn Star

24. Stitch the remaining (2) Unit Ds to the sides of Unit E, noting their orientation. Press the seams toward Unit E to make a 6½" × 12½" center unit. Clip and swirl the seams, where needed, to press flat.

 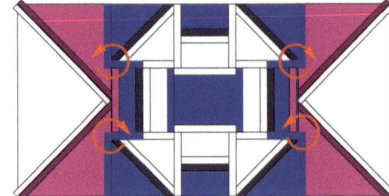

25. Stitch (2) frame units to the top and bottom of Unit E, noting orientation. Press the seams toward the frame units, to make a 12½" × 12½" block center. Clip and swirl the seams, where needed, to press flat.

26. Stitch (2) Unit Cs to the left and right of the block center, noting orientation. Press the seams toward the block center to make a 12½" × 24½" center assembly. Clip and swirl the seams, where needed, to press flat.

   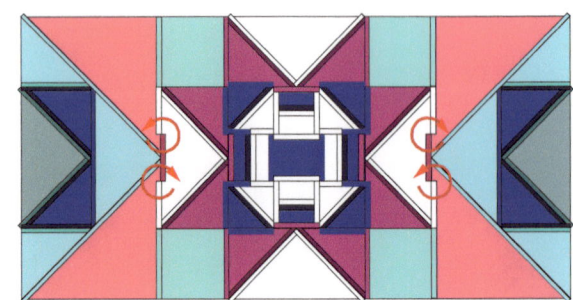

Stardust

27. Stitch (2) A/C/B units to the top and bottom of the center assembly to make a 24½" × 24½" unfinished Block 5A. Clip and swirl the seams, where needed, to press flat. Make 1.

Block 5A - Make 1

Month 5: Churn Star

Tame Those Wacky Corners!
give your quilts a unique finish without fear

available from your local independent shop or online at bindingcrazyangles.com

Month 6: Shooting Stars

Block 6A
Make 7
Finished: 6" × 6"
Unfinished: 6½" × 6½"

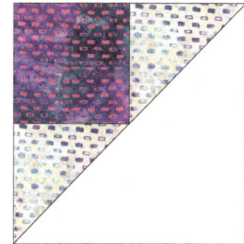

Block 6B
Make 8
Finished: 6" × 6"
Unfinished: 6½" × 6½"

Block 6C
Make 5
Finished: 6" × 6"
Unfinished: 6½" × 6½"

Cutting:

Fabric #	Fabric Swatch	Reference Illustration	Yardage
2	311902025	Lt. Cream	o Cut (2) 3⅞" × WOF strips. 　o From strips, cut (16) 3⅞" squares. Cut along one diagonal to make (32) Fabric 2 HSTs. [HST-3] o From 3⅞" × 32" strip set side in Month 5, cut (4) 3⅞" squares. Cut along one diagonal for (8) Fabric 2 HSTs. [HST-3]
3	311902360	Pink	o Cut (1) 3½" × WOF strip. 　o From strip, cut (7) 3½" Fabric 3 squares. [SQ-3]
5	311902851	Violet	o Cut (1) 3½" × WOF strip. 　o From strip, cut (8) 3½" Fabric 5 squares. [SQ-3]
14	311905585	Navy	o From 3½" × 20" strip set aside in Month 5, cut (5) 3½" Fabric 14 squares. [SQ-3]
15	SPRINKLES	Neutral	o Cut (2) 6⅞" × WOF strips. 　o From strips, cut (10) 6⅞" squares. Cut along one diagonal for (20) Fabric 15 HSTs. [HST-6]

Making Block 6A:

1. Sew the short edge of (1) Fabric 2 HST to the right side of (1) 3½" Fabric 3 square. Press the seam open.

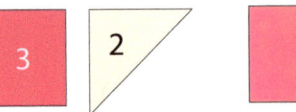
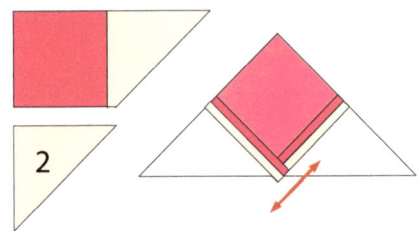

2. Sew the short edge of another Fabric 2 HST to the bottom of the Fabric 2/3 unit to make a pieced HST. Press the seam open.

3. Sew the long edge of (1) Fabric 15 HST to the pieced HST unit. Press the seam toward Fabric 15 to make a 6½" × 6½" Block 6A. Make 7.

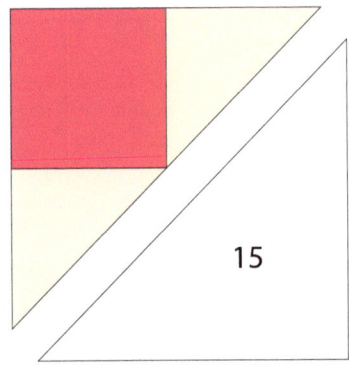

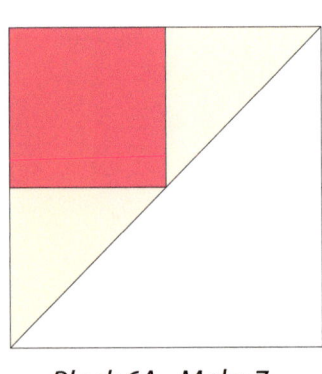

Block 6A - Make 7

Making Block 6B:

1. Sew the short edge of (1) Fabric 2 HST to the right side of (1) 3½" Fabric 5 square. Press the seam open.

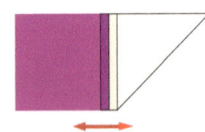

2. Sew the short edge of another Fabric 2 HST to the bottom of the Fabric 2/5 unit to make a pieced HST. Press the seam open.

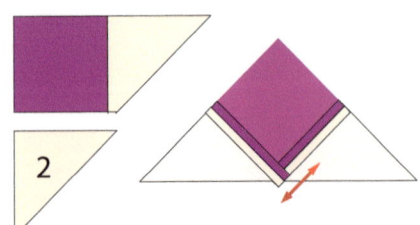

3. Sew the long edge of (1) Fabric 15 HST to the pieced HST unit. Press the seam toward Fabric 15 to make a 6½" × 6½" Block 6B. Make 8.

Block 6B - Make 8

Making Block 6C:

1. Sew the short edge of (1) Fabric 2 HST to the right side of (1) 3½" Fabric 14 square. Press the seam open.

  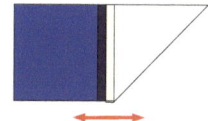

2. Sew the short edge of another Fabric 2 HST to the bottom of the Fabric 2/14 unit to make a pieced HST. Press the seam open.

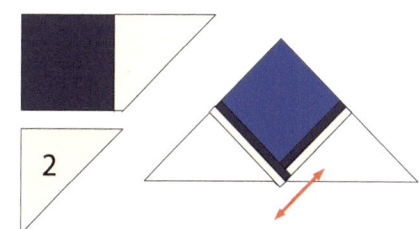

3. Sew the long edge of (1) Fabric 15 HST to the pieced HST unit. Press the seam toward Fabric 15 to make a 6½" × 6½" Block 6C. Make 5.

Block 6C - Make 5

Month 6: Shooting Stars

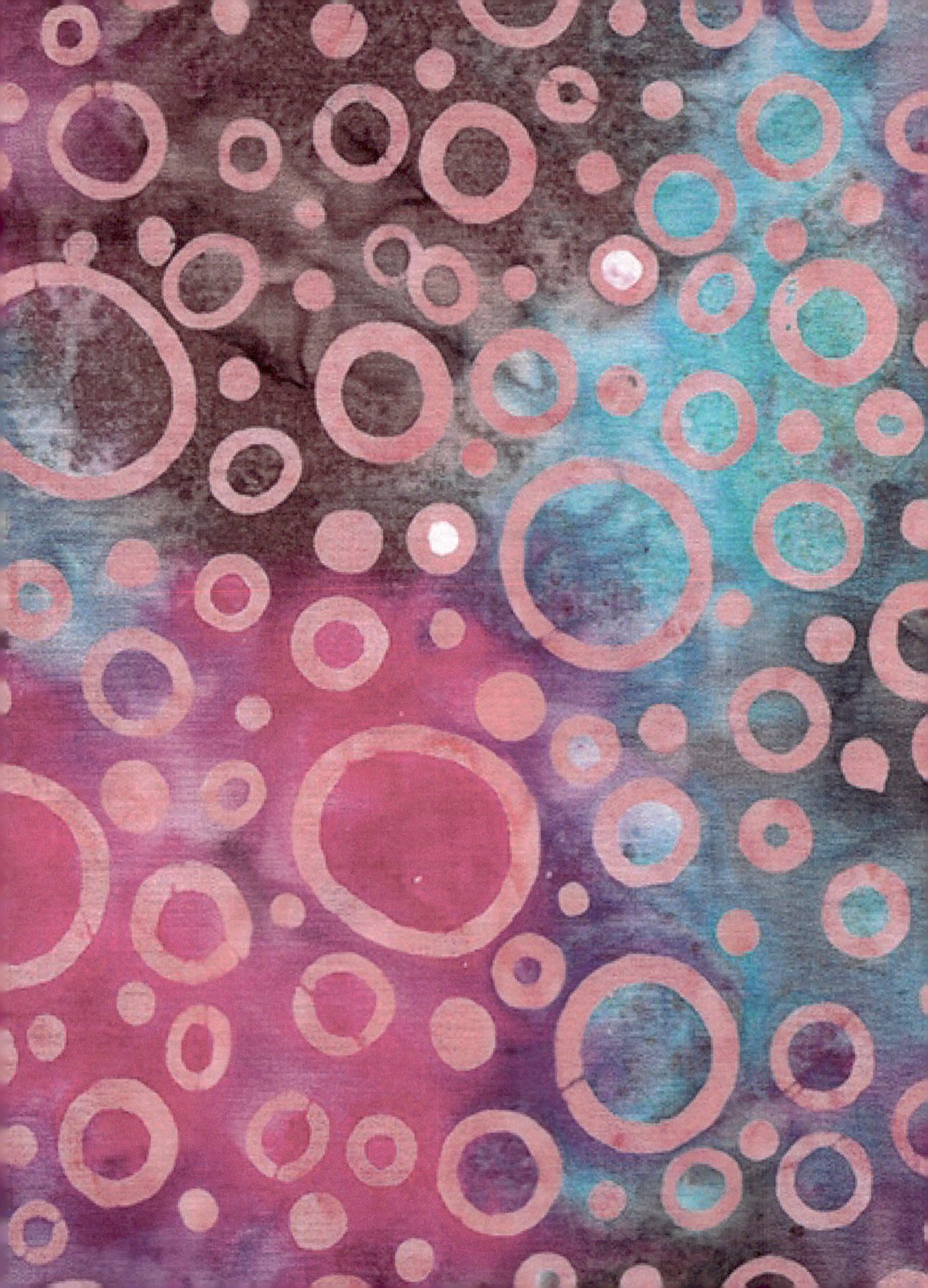

Month 7: Quilt Assembly 1

Subassembly 1
Make 1
Finished: 6" × 30"
Unfinished: 6½" × 30½"

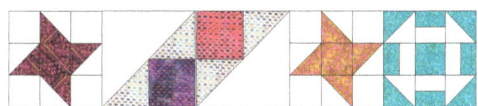

Subassembly 2
Make 1
Finished: 6" × 30"
Unfinished: 6½" × 30½"

Subassembly 3
Make 1
Finished: 12" × 18"
Unfinished: 12½" × 18½"

Subassembly 4
Make 2
Finished: 12" × 18"
Unfinished: 12½" × 18½"

Subassembly 5
Make 1
Finished: 12" × 18"
Unfinished: 12½" × 18½"

Subassembly 6
Make 1
Finished: 12" × 18"
Unfinished: 12½" × 18½"

Subassembly 7
Make 1
Finished: 12" × 12"
Unfinished: 12½" × 12½"

Cutting:

Fabric #	Fabric Swatch	Reference Illustration	Yardage
15	SPRINKLES	Neutral	o Cut (2) 3½" × WOF strips. o From strips, cut (4) 3½" × 18½" rectangles. [STR-3]

Subassembly 1:

1. Sew (1) 6A block to the right of (1) 6B block. Clip the seam allowance and press to lay flat.

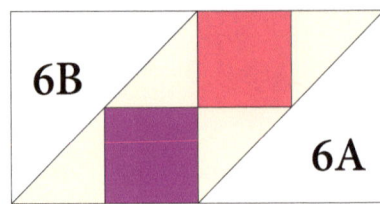

2. Sew the 6A/6B unit between (1) 2A block and (1) 2B block. Press the seams toward the 6A/6B unit.

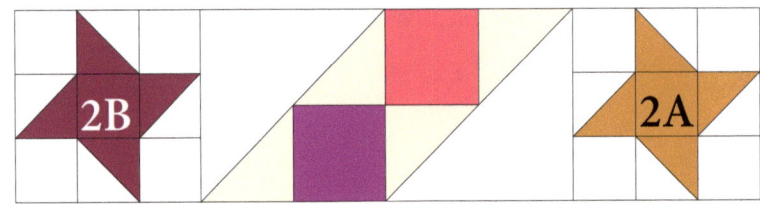

3. Sew (1) 1C block to the right end of the 2B/6B/6A/2A panel. Clip, swirl and press the seams flat and square to make a 6½" × 30½" Subassembly 1. Make 1.

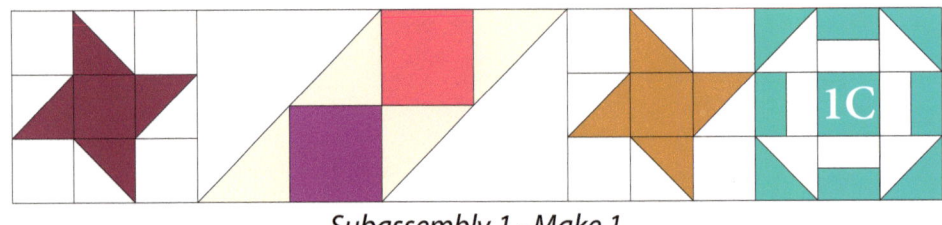

Subassembly 1 - Make 1

Subassembly 2:

1. Sew (1) 3C block to the right of (1) 3B block. Clip the seam allowance and press to lay flat.

2. Sew the 3B/3C unit between (1) 2C block and (1) 2A block. Press the seams toward the 3B/3C unit.

3. Sew (1) 1C block to the right end of the 2C/3B/3C/2A panel. Clip, swirl and press the seams flat and square to make a 6½" × 30½" Subassembly 2. Make 1.

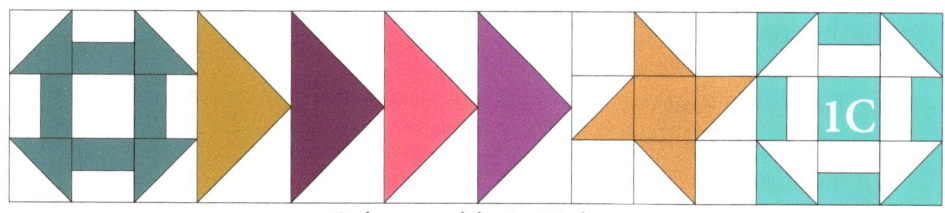

Subassembly 2 - Make 1

Subassembly 3:

1. Lay out (1) each of blocks 6A, 6C, 6B, 2C, 1C and 2A in three rows of two blocks each, noting the placement and orientation of each block.

2. Sew the blocks together in each row. Press the seams in the top and bottom rows to the right. Press the seams in the middle row to the left.

3. Join the rows. Clip, swirl and press the seams flat and square to make a 12½" × 18½" Subassembly 3. Make 1.

Subassembly 3 - Make 1

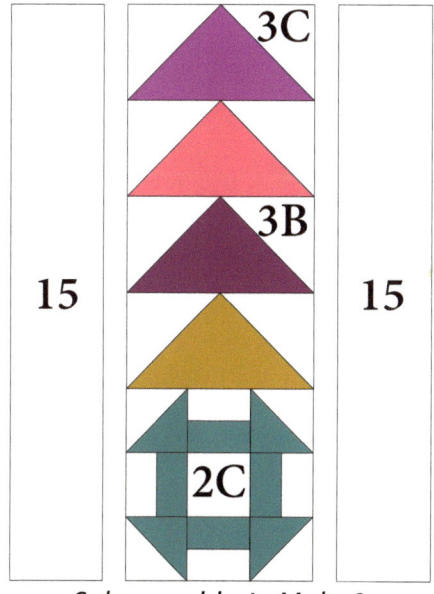

Subassembly 4 - Make 2

Subassembly 4:

1. Sew (1) 3B block between (1) 2C block and (1) 3C block as shown. Press the seams toward the 3C block.

2. Sew the 2C/3B/3C panel between (2) 3½" × 18½" Fabric 15 rectangles. Press the seams toward the Fabric 15 rectangles to make a 12½" × 18½" Subassembly 4. Make 2.

Subassembly 5:

1. Lay out (1) each of blocks 2C, 3B, 3C, 2B, 1C and 2A in two rows of three blocks each, noting the placement and orientation of each block.

2. Sew the blocks together in each row. Press the seams in the top row to the right. Press the seams in the bottom row to the left.

3. Join the rows. Clip, swirl and press the seams flat and square to make a 12½" × 18½" Subassembly 5. Make 1.

Subassembly 5 - Make 1

Subassembly 6:

1. Lay out (1) each of blocks 6A, 2C, 3B, 2A, 3C and 1C in two rows of three blocks each, noting the placement and orientation of each block.

2. Sew the blocks together in each row. Clip, swirl and press the seams flat.

3. Join the rows. Clip, swirl and press the seams flat and square to make a 12½" × 18½" Subassembly 6. Make 1.

Subassembly 6 - Make 1

Subassembly 7:

1. Lay out (1) each of blocks 2B, 6A, 6C and 6B in two rows of two blocks each, noting the placement and orientation of each block.

2. Sew the blocks together in each row. Clip, swirl and press the seams flat.

3. Join the rows. Clip, swirl and press the seams flat and square to make a 12½" × 12½" Subassembly 7. Make 1.

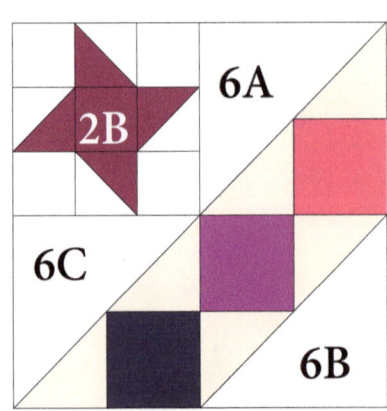

Subassembly 7 - Make 1

Month 8: Quilt Assembly 2

Subassembly 8
Make 1
Finished: 12" × 24"
Unfinished: 12½" × 24½"

Subassembly 9
Make 1
Finished: 12" × 24"
Unfinished: 12½" × 24½"

Subassembly 10
Make 1
Finished: 12" × 18"
Unfinished: 12½" × 18½"

Subassembly 11
Make 1
Finished: 12" × 18"
Unfinished: 12½" × 18½"

Subassembly 12
Make 1
Finished: 12" × 18"
Unfinished: 12½" × 18½"

Subassembly 13
Make 1
Finished: 6" × 24"
Unfinished: 6½" × 24½"

Subassembly 14
Make 1
Finished: 12" × 12"
Unfinished: 12½" × 12½"

Cutting:

Fabric #	Fabric Swatch	Reference Illustration	Yardage
15	SPRINKLES	Neutral	○ Cut (2) 3½" × WOF strips. 　　○ From strips, cut (4) 3½" × 12½" rectangles. [STR-3]

Subassembly 8:

1. Sew (1) 3A block between (2) 3½" × 12½" Fabric 15 rectangles as shown. Press the seams toward the Fabric 15 rectangles.

2. Sew (1) 2C block to the top of (1) 6A block. Press the seam toward the 6A block.

3. Sew the 2C/6A unit to the right of the 3A unit. Press the seam toward the Fabric 15 rectangle to make a 12½" × 24½" Subassembly 8. Make 1.

Subassembly 8 - Make 1

Subassembly 9:

1. Lay out (1) each of blocks 3C, 6B, 3B and 6C in two rows of two blocks each, noting the placement and orientation of each block.

2. Sew the blocks together in each row. Clip, swirl and press the seams flat.

3. Join the rows. Clip, swirl and press the seams flat and square to make a 12½" × 12½" 3C/3B/6B/6C unit.

4. Sew the 3C/3B/6B/6C unit to the right side of the 1A block. Clip, swirl and press the seams flat to make a 12½" × 24½" Subassembly 9. Make 1.

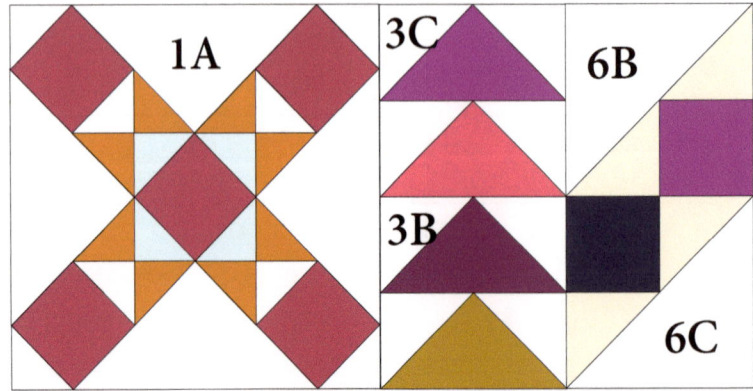

Subassembly 9 - Make 1

Stardust

Subassembly 10:

1. Sew (1) 3B block to the left side of (1) 3C block. Press the seam toward the 3C block.

2. Sew the 3B/3C unit to the top of the 1B block. Clip, swirl and press the seams flat and square to make a 12½" × 18½" Subassembly 10. Make 1.

Subassembly 10 - Make 1

Subassembly 11:

1. Lay out (1) each of blocks 6C, 6B, 2C, 3C, 3B and 1C in three rows of two blocks each, noting the placement and orientation of each block.

2. Sew the blocks together in each row. Clip, swirl and press the seams flat and square.

3. Join the rows. Clip, swirl and press the seams flat and square to make a 12½" × 18½" Subassembly 11. Make 1.

Subassembly 11 - Make 1

Subassembly 12:

1. Lay out (1) each of blocks 3C, 6B, 6A, 6C, 6B and 2B in three rows of two blocks each, noting the placement and orientation of each block.

2. Sew the blocks together in each row. Clip, swirl and press the seams flat and square.

3. Join the rows. Clip, swirl and press the seams flat and square to make a 12½" × 18½" Subassembly 12. Make 1.

Subassembly 12 - Make 1

Month 8: Quilt Assembly 2

Subassembly 13:

1. Sew (1) 3B block to the left side of (1) 3C block. Press the seam toward the 3C block.

2. Sew (1) 6B block to the left side of (1) 6A block. Clip, swirl and press the seam flat and square.

3. Sew the 3B/3C unit to the right side of the 6B/6A unit. Press the seam toward the 3B/3C unit to make a 6½" × 24½" Subassembly 13. Make 1.

Subassembly 13 - Make 1

Subassembly 14:

1. Sew (1) 2C block to the top of (1) 3B block. Clip, swirl and press the seam flat and square.

2. Sew the 2C/3B unit between (2) 3½" × 12½" Fabric 15 rectangles as shown. Press the seams toward the Fabric 15 rectangles to make a 12½" × 12½" Subassembly 14. Make 1.

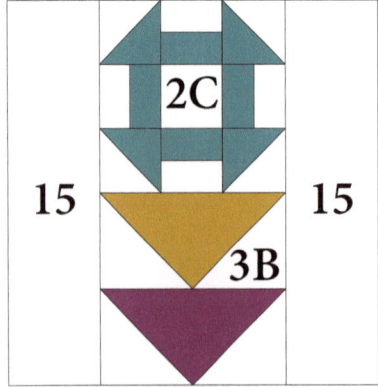

Subassembly 14 - Make 1

Month 9: Quilt Finishing

Subassembly A
Make 1
Finished: 30" × 30"
Unfinished: 30½" × 30½"

Subassembly B
Make 1
Finished: 30" × 30"
Unfinished: 30½" × 30½"

Subassembly C
Make 1
Finished: 24" × 30"
Unfinished: 24½" × 30½"

Subassembly D
Make 1
Finished: 30" × 36"
Unfinished: 30½" × 36½"

Subassembly E
Make 1
Finished: 12" × 60"
Unfinished: 12½" × 60½"

Cutting:

Fabric #	Fabric Swatch	Reference Illustration	Yardage
BINDING	311901585	Midnight	○ For ¼" finished binding: Cut (7) 2" × WOF strips. [STR-1½] **OR** ○ For ⅜" finished binding: Cut (7) 2½" × WOF strips. [STR-2]

BACKING	311902725	Med. Grey	○ Backing Option 1: Cut (2) WOF × 2¼ yard lengths, **OR**
			 ○ For Backing Option 2: Cut (1) 68½" x WOF length and (1) 44½" x WOF length.
			   ○ From the 68½" length, cut (2) 18½" x 68½" rectangles.
			   ○ From the 44½" length, cut (2) 15" x 44½" rectangles.

Subassembly A:

1. Sew Subassembly 3 to the left of block 4B. Press, clip and swirl seams as needed to press flat and square.

2. Sew Subassembly 1 to the top of the 3/4B assembly. Press, clip and swirl seams as needed to press flat and square.

3. Sew Subassembly 2 to the bottom of the 3/1/4B assembly. Press, clip and swirl seams as needed to press flat and square to make a 30½" × 30½" Subassembly A.

Subassembly B:

1. Sew Subassembly 4 to the top of Subassembly 7. Press, clip and swirl seams as needed to press flat and square.

2. Sew Subassembly 5 to the top of block 4A. Press, clip and swirl seams as needed to press flat and square.

3. Sew the 4/7 assembly to the 5/4A assembly. Press, clip and swirl seams as needed to press flat and square to make a 30½" × 30½" Subassembly B.

Subassembly C:

1. Sew Subassembly 10 to the left of Subassembly 11. Press, clip and swirl seams as needed to press flat and square.

2. Sew Subassembly 8 to the top of the 10/11 assembly. Press, clip and swirl seams as needed to press flat and squareto make a 24½" × 30½" Subassembly C.

Stardust

Subassembly D:

1. Sew Subassembly 13 to the top of block 5A. Press, clip and swirl seams as needed to press flat and square.
2. Sew Subassembly 14 to the top of Subassembly 12. Press, clip and swirl seams as needed to press flat and square.
3. Sew the 13/5A assembly to the 14/12 assembly. Press, clip and swirl seams as needed to press flat and square to make a 30½" × 36½" Subassembly D.

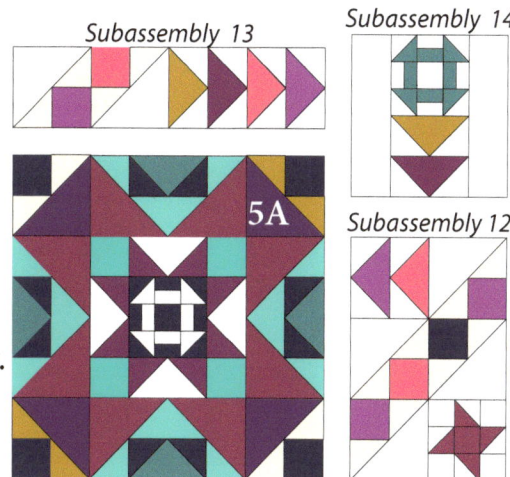

Subassembly E:

1. Sew Subassembly 4 to the left of Subassembly 9. Press, clip and swirl seams as needed to press flat and square.
2. Sew Subassembly 6 to the right of the 4/9 assembly. Press, clip and swirl seams as needed to press flat and square to make a 12½" × 60½" Subassembly E.

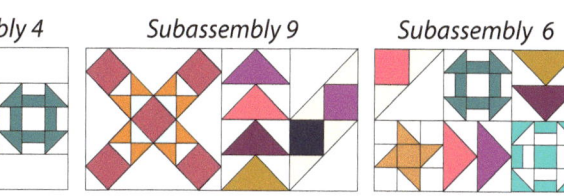

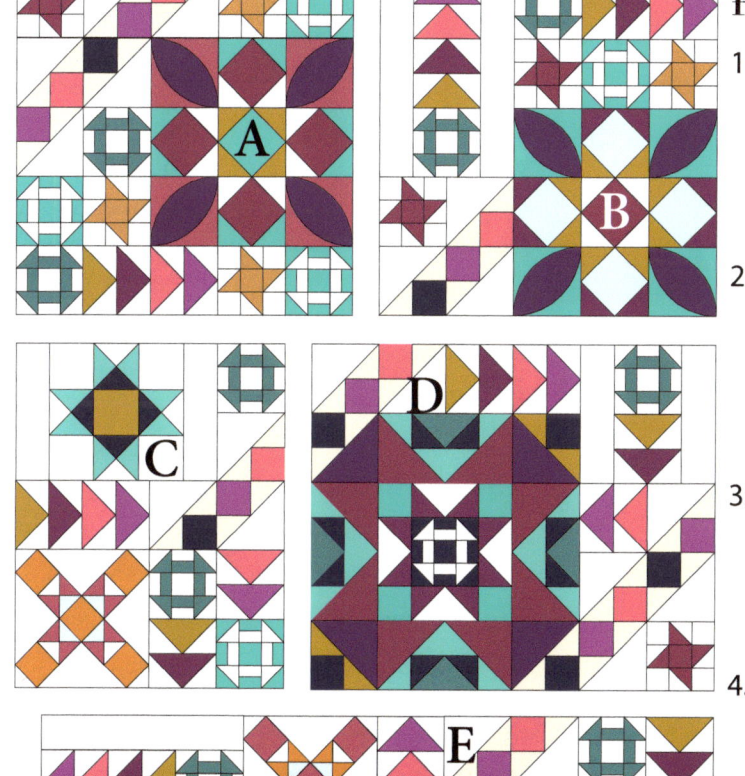

Final Assembly:

1. Sew Subassembly A to the left of Subassembly B. Press, clip and swirl seams as needed to press flat and square to make the top row of the quilt.
2. Sew Subassembly C to the left of Subassembly D. Press, clip and swirl seams as needed to press flat and square to make the middle row of the quilt.
3. Sew the A/B assembly to the top of the C/D assembly. Press, clip and swirl seams as needed to press flat and square.
4. Sew Subassembly E to the bottom of the A/B/C/D assembly. Press, clip and swirl seams as needed to press flat and square to make a 60½" × 72½" quilt top.

Backing Option 1:

1. Trim the selvage edges from each of the (2) WOF × 2¼ yard lengths of backing.

2. Using a ½" seam allowance, sew the long sides of the (2) lengths together to make a large backing panel. Press seams to one side.

3. Trim the backing so that it measures approximately 68" × 80". Offset your seam so that it is not exactly in the center of the backing. This will help reduce the wear on your backing seam if you have a tendency to fold your quilts in half.

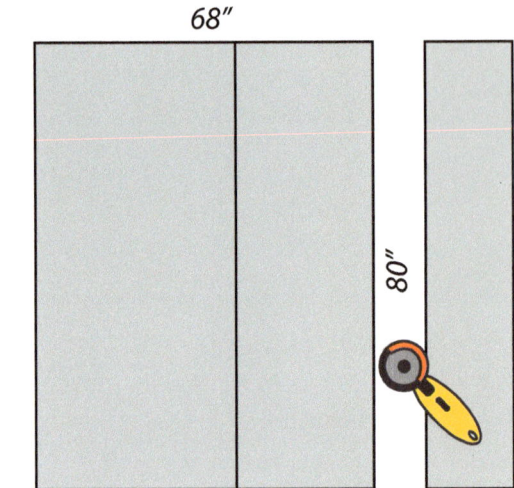

Backing Option 2:

If you would prefer to piece your backing from scraps, there are many possibilities! One simple option is detailed here. Feel free to make whatever backing you prefer.

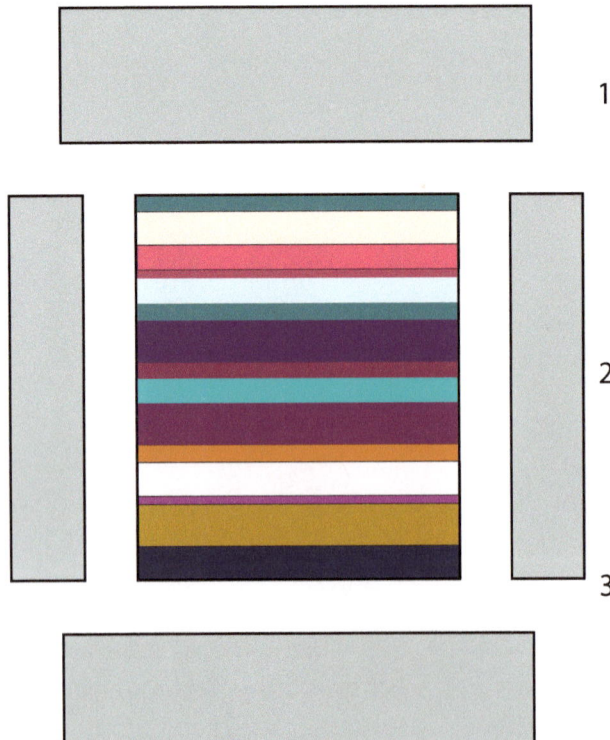

1. Cut the leftover scraps into the widest strips you can × 39½", then piece them into a strip set using a ¼" seam allowance. By our calculations, you should be able to make a strip set approximately 39½" × 44½" from the leftover scraps.

2. Sew the scrap panel between (2) 15" × 44½" backing rectangles. Press seams toward the backing rectangles to make a 44½" × 68½" center panel.

3. Sew the center panel between (2) 18½" × 68½" backing rectangles. Press seams toward the backing rectangles. Square up the backing to make a 68" × 80" scrappy backing.

Making the Binding:

1. Sew (7) binding strips together end to end using a 90° diagonal seam. Lay strip #1 on a flat surface, right side up. Place strip #2 on the end of strip #1, right sides together at a 90° angle.

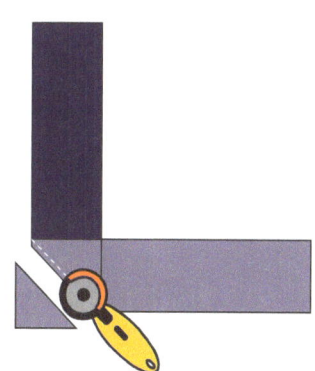

2. Sew the strips together diagonally, starting at the top left corner and ending on the bottom right corner as shown. Trim the seam to ¼" and press the seam open.

3. Repeat using the remaining (5) binding strips, trimming and pressing the seams open to make a long binding strip.

4. Fold the long binding strip in half widthwise, wrong sides together, and press well.

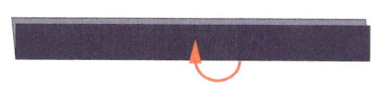

Finishing:

1. Layer the backing, the batting and the quilt top and baste the layers using your favorite method.

2. Quilt as desired! We used a digital edge-to-edge design called *EZ Doodle Set #3* by Karlee Porter, but you could also do free motion or walking foot quilting.

3. Before you trim the excess batting and backing from your quilt, stay-stitch using a long basting stitch ⅛" from the edge through all three layers. This will help secure your quilt top for binding.

4. Bind your quilt using your favorite method. If you'd like to learn how to give your quilts a great looking binding completely by machine, get the book *Get It Done Now! Binding a Quilt by Machine, 2nd Edition,* also by Ebony Love.

Backing *(wrong side up)*
Batting
Quilt *(right side up)*

Month 9: Quilt Finishing

Stardust

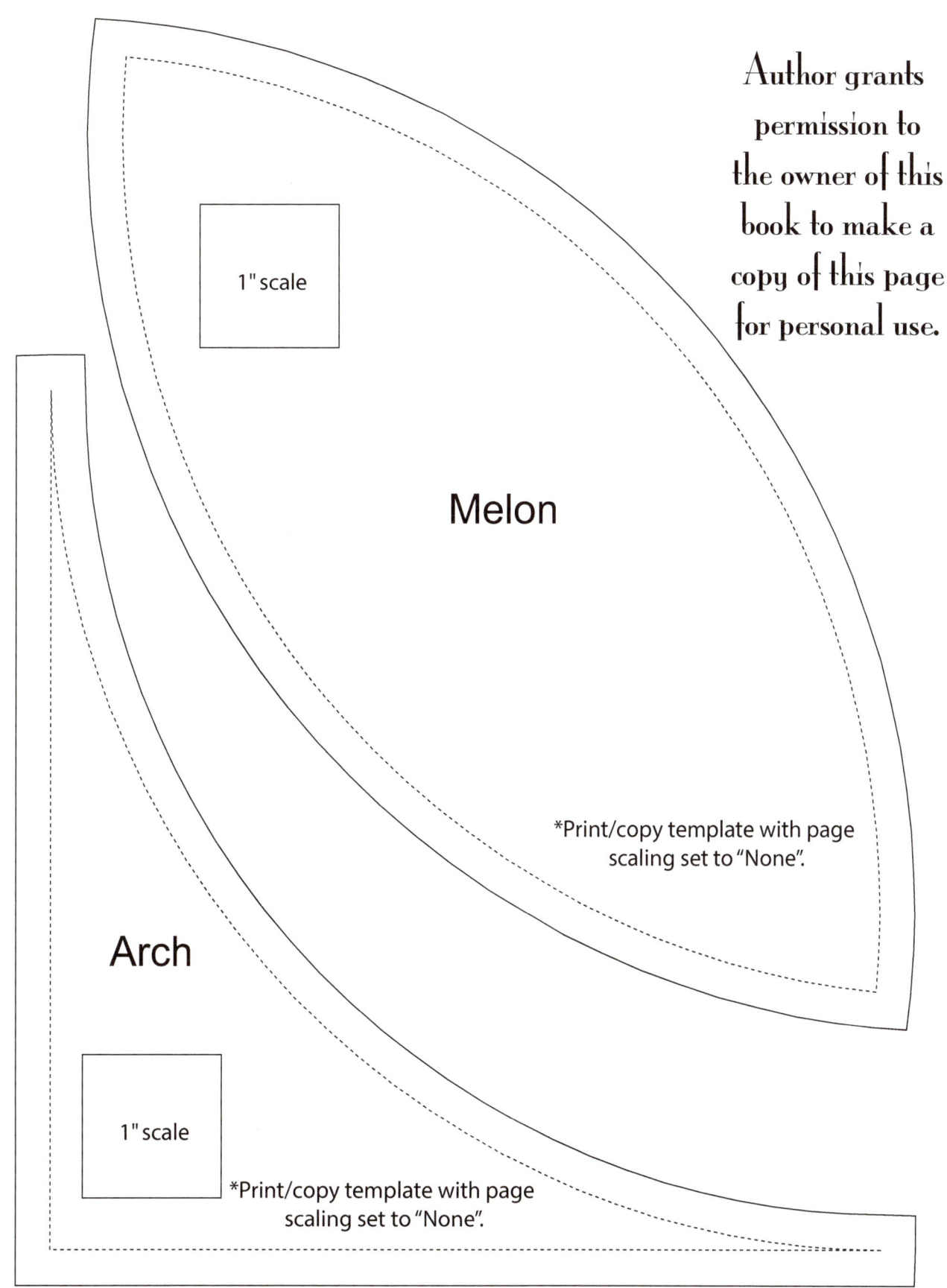

This page is intentionally left blank.

Supply List

Notions

- Patchwork Glasshead Pins, Size 30
- Aurifil 50wt Mako Cotton Thread #2310 Light Beige
    - Used for piecing & quilting
- Aurifil 50wt Mako Cotton Thread #4241 Very Dark Grey
    - Used for binding

Rulers

- Easy Angle Tool 6½"
    - The 10½" Easy Angle Ruler also works
- Companion Angle Triangle Ruler
    - This can cut quarter-square triangles up to 10" finished
- Corner Trimmer by Marti Michell
    - Trims the corner of triangles to help with alignment of rotary cut units
- Orange Peel Template Set by LoveBug Studios
    - A paper template is also supplied with the pattern

Die Cutting

We use the Equivalent Die Notation (EDeN) System for notating patterns. For more information or to download a full chart, visit **http://equivalentdienotation.com**

- **EDeN Numbers:** HST-2, HST-3, HST-6, QST-4, QST-6, QST-8, REC-1x2, SOP-4, SOP-6, SQ-2, SQ-3, SQ-4, STR-1, STR-1½, STR-2, STR-3
- **Other Dies:** Orange Peel Sizzix Die (662531)

Binding

These items may be helpful if you want to bind your quilt by machine.

- Get It Done Now! Binding a Quilt by Machine, 2nd Edition
- LoveBug Studios Binding Tool
- Chaco Liner Chalk Pen

All supplies are optional unless otherwise noted.

EDeN™ System Chart

EDeN™ Number (finished size)	Rotary (cut size)	Sizzix®	AccuQuilt GO®	AccuQuilt Studio™
HST-2	Cut a 2-7/8" square; cut in half along one diagonal (makes 2)	656685, 657611, 659831—Sizzix Die—Half-Square Triangles, 2 1/2" Finished Square	55018, 55021—Value Die (2 1/2" Triangles) OR 55063—GO! Half Square—2" Finished Triangle Multiples, 55712 - 8" QUBE Shape 5	50161, 50272—Studio Half Square—2" Finished Triangle
HST-3	Cut a 3-7/8" square; cut in half along one diagonal (makes 2)	656686, 657612—Sizzix Die—Half-Square Triangles, 3 1/2" Finished Square	55009—GO! Half Square—3" Finished Triangle, 55703 - 6" QUBE Shape 3, 12" QUBE Shape 5 OR 55048—GO! Bountiful Baskets (3 1/2" cut)	50163, 50278—Studio Half Square—3" Finished Triangle
HST-6	Cut a 6-7/8" square; cut in half along one diagonal (makes 2)	657638— Sizzix Die—Half-Square Triangles, 6 1/2" Finished Square	55001—GO! Triangle 6 1/2", 12" QUBE Shape 3	50033, 50276—Studio Half Square—6" Finished Triangle
QST-4	Cut a 5-1/4" square; cut in half along both diagonals (makes 4)	657614—Sizzix Originals Die—Triangle, 2 5/8"H x 4 1/2"W Unfinished OR 657166, 659852—Sizzix Die—Triangles, 2 1/2"H x 4 1/2"W Unfinished	55047, 55316—GO! Quarter Square 4" Finished Triangles, 55711 - 8" QUBE Shape 4	50271, 50365—Studio Quarter Square—4" Finished Triangle
QST-6	Cut a 7-1/4" square; cut in half along both diagonals (makes 4)	657621—Sizzix Clear Die—Triangle, 3 5/8"H x 6 1/2"W Unfinished OR 657171, 661650 —Sizzix Die—Triangles, 3 1/2"H x 6 1/2"W Unfinished	55002—GO! Triangle 4 7/8", 55726 - 12" QUBE Shape 4	50034, 50277—Studio Quarter Square—6" Finished Triangle
QST-8	Cut a 9-1/4" square; cut in half along both diagonals (makes 4)	657639—Sizzix Bigz XL Die—Triangle, 4 5/8"H x 8 1/2"W Unfinished OR 657172—Sizzix Die—Triangles, 4 1/2"H x 8 1/2"W Unfinished	55399—GO! Quarter Square 8" Finished Triangle	50790—Studio Quarter Square—8" Finished Triangle
REC-1 x 2	Cut a strip 2-1/2" wide; subcut to 1-1/2"	STR-2 AND STR-1	STR-2 AND STR-1	STR-2 AND STR-1
SOP-4	Cut a strip 3-5/16" wide; subcut to 3-5/16"	NONE	55317—GO! Square—3 1/4", 55713 - 8" QUBE Shape 6 (use a scant 1/4" seam)	50128—Studio Square on Point – 3 1/4"

© LoveBug Studios, 2011-2020. You may freely copy these charts for personal use only. Full versions available on http://equivalentdie.com

EDeN™ System Chart

EDeN™ Number (finished size)	Rotary (cut size)	Sizzix®	AccuQuilt GO!®	AccuQuilt Studio™
SOP-6	Cut a strip 4-3/4" wide; subcut to 4-3/4"	NONE	55019—GO! Square—4 3/4", 55725 - 12" QUBE Shape 6	50035, 50144—Studio Square on Point—4 3/4"
SQ-2	Cut a strip 2-1/2" wide; subcut to 2-1/2"	656674, 656682, 657607—Sizzix Die—Squares, 2" Finished OR STR-2	55059—GO! Square 2 1/2" Multiples, 55709 - 8" QUBE Shape 2 OR 55018, 55021 – Value Die (2 1/2" Square) OR STR-2	50124, 50204, 50603—Studio Square—2 1/2" OR STR-2
SQ-3	Cut a strip 3-1/2" wide; subcut to 3-1/2"	656683, 657608—Sizzix Die—Squares, 3" Finished OR STR-3	55006—GO! Square 3 1/2", 55701 – 6" QUBE Shape 1, 12" QUBE Shape 2 OR STR-3	50140, 50206—Studio Square—3 1/2" OR STR-3
SQ-4	Cut a strip 4-1/2" wide; subcut to 4-1/2"	657609—Sizzix Bigz Die—Square, 4" Finished OR STR-4	55018, 55021—Value Die (4 1/2" Square) OR 55060—GO! Square—4 1/2" Multiples, 55708 - 8" QUBE Shape 1 OR STR-4	50015, 50123 – Studio Square—4 1/2" OR STR-4
STR-1	Cut a LOF strip X 1-1/2" wide	656680—Sizzix Bigz XL 25" Die—Strips, 1 1/2" Wide use the lengthwise grain for borders	55024, 55075—GO! Strip Cutter 1 1/2" OR 55164—GO! Strip Cutter—1", 1 1/2", 2" (use 1 1/2" strip) use the lengthwise grain for borders	50052, 50065—Studio Strip Cutter 1 1/2" use the lengthwise grain for borders
STR-1½	Cut a LOF strip X 2" wide	657633, 656687—Sizzix Die—Strips, 2" Wide use the lengthwise grain for borders	55025, 55073—GO! Strip Cutter 2" OR 55164—GO! Strip Cutter—1", 1 1/2", 2" (use 2" strip) use the lengthwise grain for borders	50054, 50611—Studio Strip Cutter—2" use the lengthwise grain for borders
STR-2	Cut a LOF strip X 2-1/2" wide	656681, 656688, 658328, 658330—Sizzix Die—Strips, 2 1/2" Wide use the lengthwise grain for borders	55014, 55017—GO! Strip Cutter 2 1/2" use the lengthwise grain for borders	50056, 50612—Studio Strip Cutter 2 1/2" use the lengthwise grain for borders
STR-3	Cut a LOF strip X 3-1/2" wide	656689, 657898—Sizzix Die—Strips, 3 1/2" Wide use the lengthwise grain for borders	55032, 55074—GO! Strip Cutter—3 1/2" use the lengthwise grain for borders	50011, 50060—Studio Strip Cutter—3 1/2" use the lengthwise grain for borders

© LoveBug Studios, 2011-2020. You may freely copy these charts for personal use only. Full versions available on http://equivalentdienotation.com

EDeN™ Chart

Other Block of the Month Patterns
designed by Ebony Love

A Garden for All Seasons
by Ebony Love

In the south with its warm weather and gentle breezes, flowers bloom year-round, but the state flowers which bloom from January to June have something special about them.

This heady season begins with the white camellia in Alabama, and takes us through the bright pink azaleas of Georgia.

Shades of Saxony
by Ebony Love

Among the venerable avenues in Britain, you'll find majestic cathedrals dominating the landscape all around the province of Canterbury.

Inspired by images of the Cathedral Church of St. Mary in Truro, the Cathedral Church of St. Martin in Leicester, and others, Shades of Saxony is a quilted adventure exploring these awe-inspiring monuments of faith.

Carnivale
by Ebony Love

Inspired by visions of fun and frivolity, embark on the colorful journey that is Carnivale!

Bright colors and interesting shapes abound in this twist on traditional quilt blocks in a modern, vibrant color palette.

available from your local independent shop or online at LoveBugStudios.com

www.ingramcontent.com/pod-product-compliance
Lightning Source LLC
Chambersburg PA
CBHW041832300426

44111CB00002B/63